MONEY TALK

Building Wealth
Through Passive Income

TIERRE FORD

TIERRE FORD

Disclaimer

This book is a work of insight, experience, and research. The strategies, numbers, and examples presented are drawn from real-world observations and documented sources within the sports and business industries. While every effort has been made to provide accurate, practical, and inspiring content, results may vary based on individual effort, timing, circumstances, and application. This book is not a promise—it's a blueprint. Your success depends on how you build with it.

About The Author

At just 12 years old, I started selling drugs in the 6th grade—following the blueprint I saw in my own home. My father was both a dealer and a user, and by the 7th grade, I had bought my first car, was paying my mama rent, and buying my own school clothes.

That same year, the school system labeled me as "slow." They placed me in a remedial reading class—embarrassed me, honestly. I was ashamed. But I still kept my swag, my gold chains, my Starter jackets, and my game face. I was one of the most popular kids in school, but truth be told, I had stopped learning. I was only there to show off.

Then one day, my reading teacher—who I'll never forget—looked me in my eyes and said, "You don't belong in this class. You're smart. Don't let them label you." Her words stuck with me, even though my CRT test scores said otherwise.

At age 12 years old I became my neighborhood's youngest drug supplier. I started with 10 dollars, and I flipped that all the way to over $500,000. Me and my Dad link up dealing together supplying the market. I dropped out of high school in the 10th grade. I bought my mother a house with a pool in the backyard, purchased luxury cars, before I was locked up at 19.

At that point in my life, I had never read a full book. Not one. But my father always told me, **"The mind is the most powerful tool in the universe. Street sense and book sense together? That's unstoppable."**

So I gave books a chance.

It started with street fiction. Then history. Then business. Then biographies about powerful and wealthy people. I started seeing myself in those pages—not always in their polish, but in their ambition, their boldness. Then I read **Think and Grow Rich and As a Man Thinketh.** Those two books changed my entire mindset.

That's when I met my friend Cool Harris. I saw some of his writing on a notepad, and it rocked my world. I realized I had something to say, too. From that moment on, I picked up the pencil—and I've never looked back.

I earned my GED, took business and college courses, and started studying resilience. I discovered that, back in the day, Black people were once forbidden to read. There's even a saying: **"If you want to hide something from a Black person, put it in a book."** That became my fuel.

Now, I write both fiction and self-help books, covering everything from mindset and mental toughness to financial strategy and spiritual growth. I pour my soul into every page with one mission: to light a fire inside someone who's ready for change.

To everyone who's followed my journey—thank you. Let's set the world on fire with truth, with courage, with knowledge. Let's break every chain and every myth that says we don't read.

Peace—And Keep The Faith.

TIERRE FORD

Author's Message

For Those Who Made It. Lost It. Or Still Chasing It.

This book was written from the trenches—from real experiences, real lessons, and real losses. I come from the hustle. I've seen uncles, brothers, friends—smart men—stack hundreds of thousands, even millions. Only to give most of it back. To lawyers. Bonds. The feds. Or the streets that once cheered for them.

It ain't just about making money. It's what you do **after** you make it. I watched too many go in shining and come home to nothing. Why? Because the money stopped when they did. Time becomes your enemy when you gotta earn every dollar with sweat, risk, or sacrifice.

This book is for:

- **The hustlers** who learned the hard way.
- **The nine-to-fivers** who feel like the goalpost moves every time they get close.
- **The grinders** who think they don't earn enough to save.
- And **the dreamers** who know there's more, but need the blueprint.

Let's be clear—**you don't need a million to build wealth**. You need understanding. Discipline. Patience. A shift in mindset. Because when you start making your money work for you—*while you sleep, while you're at your kids' games, or on vacation*—that's when you stop surviving and start building.

This ain't shoebox money. This ain't fast cash. This is about breaking cycles and creating new lanes.

Small moves become empires.

Smart plays become freedom.

And the compound effect? It's real.

This book ain't theory—it's **financial truth in a language the streets, the grind, and the come-up can understand.** A starting point. A mirror. A warning. A guide.

Let it put you on a new path.

Because numbers don't lie.

And wealth don't wait.

TIERRE FORD

TABLE OF CONTENTS

Copyright

Author's Message

Chapter 1

Breaking The Surface

"It's not your salary that makes you rich, it's your spending habits." — Charles A. Jaffe

They told you to get it by any means. So you did.

You stacked fast, flipped quicker, and dodged everything the block threw your way. You learned how to turn nothing into something—without investors, advisors, or a safety net. That alone makes you more brilliant than you're told. But here's the cold truth: most hustlers never make it past the surface.

Why? Because nobody showed you how money *really* works.

Every day, someone takes a major risk to get paid. They risk freedom. Risk their life. Risk everything just to hit a big lick or to build a steady street income—only to lose it all behind one wrong move, one knock at the door, or one jealous phone call. But the *real loss* happens long before that. It happens when every dollar made is stashed in a shoebox, or blown on things that don't grow value.

Luxury cars. Designer clothes. Jewelry that shines but don't appreciate.
That's not wealth.
That's *weight*—and it slows you down when the storm hits.

Assets grow. Liabilities glow. One pays you over time. The other just pays attention to you… until it doesn't.

Let's be honest: the system was never built for you to win.
But it's not just the system—it's the *lack of game*.

You might have six figures under your mattress, but no paper trail. That means no protection, no generational transfer, and no proof of wealth. You can't borrow against it. You can't multiply it. You can't even insure it. That's how the game keeps you in check: you get money, but you don't grow it.

That's what we changing today.

This ain't about judging where your money came from. It's about making sure it don't die where it started. If you're risking your life to earn, you deserve to *keep* what you earned. That starts with understanding the basic difference:

- Money working for you vs. you working for money.
- Compound growth vs. constant hustle.
- Long-term tax games vs. short-term flash.

Too many hustlers think they broke the system just by making fast money. But the truth is, you've only cracked the surface. The *real break* happens when you learn how to flip that street money into *silent money*.
The kind that grows while you sleep.
The kind that funds your kids' kids.
The kind that can't be kicked in, raided, or frozen.

You don't need millions to start. You just need *information.*
The right kind. At the right time. And used the right way.

Because in this new age—the *age of fast information*—every second counts. But every *decision* is what builds wealth. This book is for the ones who are done gambling with their freedom. Done losing everything they built in one night. And done watching everyone else talk about "generational wealth" while they still trying to survive.

Wisdom of Overcoming

You were taught how to survive the block. Now it's time to master the board.
What you're holding in your hands isn't just a book—it's a *blueprint.*
Every chapter is a key. Every formula is a weapon. Every breakdown is a breakthrough.

And it starts here.
By turning the hustle into a *harvest..*

Chapter 2

The Wealthzee Triangle – Active, Passive, And Portfolio Income

"Never depend on a single income. Invest to create a second source." — Warren Buffett

They say money is power. But not all money is created equal.

The fast money you hustle for? That's called active income.
The quiet money that comes in while you sleep? That's passive income.
And the wealth that grows from owning real parts of real things—like stocks, crypto, real estate, or businesses? That's portfolio income.

Together, they make up what I call the Wealthzee Triangle—the three sides of financial power that every boss, mogul, and legacy builder needs to understand. You master this triangle, you stop chasing the bag and start *controlling* it.

Let's break it down street-level:

1. ACTIVE INCOME – You Gotta Move to Eat

This is what most of us grow up on. From flipping packs to punching clocks, this is money that only shows up when *you do*. If you don't move, you don't eat. Doesn't matter if you're making $12 an hour or $10,000 a night—if you stop, the money stops too.

And while active income can feel powerful—especially when it's fast—it's the most dangerous to depend on. Because it *owns your time*. You miss a day, you miss a play. Your body break down, you break down the bag.

You work for the money. The money doesn't work for you.

But don't get it twisted—active income *starts* the game. It's what funds the other sides of the triangle. It's your fuel. The problem is most people *never upgrade*. They stay stuck in motion, chasing, hustling, burning out.

That's why we level up.

2. PASSIVE INCOME – Money That Moves Without You

Imagine getting paid *every week* without lifting a finger. That's passive income.

This can come from real estate rent, royalties, vending machines, digital products, content monetization, or licensing. But the key is: you build it once, and it pays you over and over.

Now don't let the word "passive" fool you. It takes *work upfront.* You gotta study. Set it up right. Avoid scams. But once it's rolling? It's freedom. It's breathing room. It's peace.

Think about it: when your bills are paid before you even wake up, you stop being desperate. You stop taking dumb risks. You get *options.*

Here's the kicker—most hustlers could build passive income *right now* with what they already know. You know how to sell? Start a course. You know how to flip? Teach the formula. You got connections? Leverage them into a business partnership.

But instead, too many cats sit on million-dollar knowledge while they burn out chasing thousand-dollar plays.

3. PORTFOLIO INCOME – Let Your Money Multiply Itself

This is where wealth *really* lives. Stocks, bonds, crypto, real estate portfolios, silent partnerships—this is ownership money. Money that makes more money by being invested.

You don't touch it every day. It grows over time. It compounds. It builds legacy.

Now I know what some of y'all thinking: *"I don't trust the stock market. I don't know real estate like that."* And that's fair. But ignorance ain't protection. Not knowing keeps you broke. Learning protects your paper.

Here's what the rich understand: portfolio income is the bridge between survival and freedom.
It's what buys time. Buys land. Buys generational peace.

The goal isn't just to hustle forever. The goal is to make your *active income feed your passive income*, and then funnel your *passive income into portfolio income*.

That's the Wealthzee Triangle:

- Work for money.
- Let money work without you.
- Let money build more money.

Now ask yourself this real question:
Where are you in the triangle?

Are you still sweating every dollar?
Are you building passive plays?
Are you putting your money to work like you do?

Most people never even *hear* these terms. But that ain't your story no more. You got the map now. And once you understand the Wealthzee Triangle, you stop playing checkers and start playing chess.

Wisdom of Overcoming

The streets teach you to grind. This triangle teaches you to *grow*.

You survived risk, pressure, betrayal, and the weight of carrying everything on your back. That means you already got the *mindset* of a boss. What you need now is the *model*. The structure. The long game.

Remember this: Fast money without a wealth system is like water in your hands—it slips away every time.

But when you learn how to channel that water—build pipes, create flow, and store it properly—you stop surviving and start thriving. You stop making it for the moment and start *building it for life*.

This is just the beginning. The streets gave you hustle.
Now let's build your freedom.

Chapter 3

Time Is A Currency – Understanding 10, 20, And 30-Year Growth Timelines

"The best time to plant a tree was 20 years ago. The second-best time is now." — **Chinese Proverb**

You ever hear somebody say, *"I ain't got time"?*
But the truth is—they just don't know what time *really is.* Time ain't just what's on your watch or your phone screen. Time is a currency, and it might be the most valuable one we have.

Money can come and go. You can lose it, flip it, get it back. But time? Once it's gone, it's gone forever. So the smartest people—the real bosses and builders—treat time like an *investment.* Not just a clock.

See, in the hustle game, we're trained to focus on the now. The quick flip. The instant result. That dopamine hit of a bag dropped today. But the wealthy? They play the long game. They think in years, not days.

That's the real shift we gotta make if we want to turn fast money into forever money.

The 10-Year Vision – From Survival To Strategy

Let's start with the next 10 years. That might sound far, but blink twice, and a decade's gone. Think about where you were 10 years ago. Think about what you *could* have done if you knew what you know now.

Now flip that: What if 10 years from now, you looked back and realized you made the *best* moves of your life starting today?

The 10-year plan is about escaping the cycle.

- You stop trading time for money.
- You start buying freedom.
- You start making your money grow roots.

This is the perfect window to lock in passive income—a rental property, a digital business, a small franchise, dividend stocks. Something that doesn't require *your* presence every day to earn. You plant those seeds now, and 10 years from now they feed you.

Don't worry if it don't start big.
Compounding turns crumbs into cakes.

The 20-Year Vision – From Money To Meaning

Twenty years out might seem wild to think about, especially if you're used to living day by day. But hear this: every empire was built brick by brick, year by year. The 20-year plan is where the game gets serious. It's no longer about just you—it's about your family, your last name, your impact.

If you start investing $500/month right now with an average 10% return (index funds, solid ETFs), in 20 years you'll be sitting on over $300,000—off a move most people *ignore.*

But more than numbers, this is when you can:

- Fully retire from the grind.
- Own your home outright.
- Have multiple income streams from assets you set up 10 years earlier.
- Pass something *real* to your kids—not just lessons, but leverage.

This ain't fantasy. It's math. It's structure. And it's discipline.

You don't get there by luck. You get there by honoring time and using it like a tool, not treating it like an enemy.

The 30-Year Vision – From Hustler To Heir

Thirty years out might feel like another lifetime. But that's the whole point. This is how generational wealth is really built. Not in a flash—but over consistent, focused effort.

The streets teach you to live for today because tomorrow ain't promised. But that mindset is exactly why we keep starting over. Our communities are stuck in "get it, spend it, run it up, crash out, repeat."

You want to change that? You want to break that cycle?

Then you need to ask:

- What's my 30-year legacy?

- Will I still be remembered for a hustle… or for building something that lasted?

In 30 years, you could own multiple real estate properties paid in full. You could have a trust set up that kicks out tax-free income to your children. You could fund a school, a program, a nonprofit in your name. You could still be getting paid off moves you made when you were 30, 40, 50—because you played the long game.

Time is the one currency we all start equal with—but most people waste it chasing money, instead of making money chase them.

The difference between broke and wealthy isn't just information. It's how long you're willing to wait. It's how far ahead you can see while everyone else is blinded by the moment.

That's why this book ain't just about fast plays—it's about *forever moves.*

Wisdom of Overcoming

You already survived what was meant to break you.
You already built something from nothing.
Now imagine what you could do if you gave yourself time to *grow it.*

The same patience you used to sit on the block, to grind through hard times, to wait for a package to land—that's the same patience that builds an empire. But now, instead of waiting on something to drop, you're planting something to rise.

The next 10, 20, 30 years of your life ain't promised—but they are *possible.*
And they can be powerful—if you use your time like a boss, not a victim.

Clock's ticking. But this time, it's ticking *for* you.

Chapter 4

Tax Strategies For Wealth Builders

"It's not what you earn that makes you rich. It's what you keep."
— **Robert Kiyosaki**

Let's keep it real—taxes ain't just for the rich. They're for the smart.

Most hustlers don't fear the streets. They fear the IRS.

Why? Because nobody taught us the tax game. We weren't raised to think in deductions, write-offs, or shelters. We were raised thinking taxes were punishment. But the truth is: taxes are a tool. And if you know how to use that tool, it won't cut you—it'll *protect* you.

The rich don't dodge taxes by hiding. They dodge taxes by *understanding the rules*. They study the code. They build structures. They hire experts. But most importantly? They move like a business, not like an individual.

That's where it starts. So let's break this down.

1. Think Like a Business, Not a Consumer

The government rewards builders. If you create jobs, own property, or invest in the economy, the IRS wants to help you keep more of your money. Not out of kindness—but because you're useful to the system.

So here's the golden rule:
If you're making money, you should be doing it through a business structure.

That means:

- Set up an LLC or S Corp.
- Keep your business and personal expenses separate.
- Get a business bank account and use it.
- Track every dollar you earn and spend.

The moment you move like a business, your entire life becomes more strategic. That laptop? Business write-off. That trip to meet a supplier? Deductible. That home office, gas mileage, marketing, phone plan? All tax tools—if your money flows through the right channel.

You can't play the game if you're not even on the field.
Form the entity. Keep the records. File like a boss.

2. Use Deductions Like Shields

The tax code in America is thick for a reason. It's not just instructions—it's a menu of what you're allowed to deduct, if you qualify.

Here's what most wealth builders legally write off:

- Home office expenses

- Internet and phone bills

- Health insurance premiums

- Vehicle mileage (especially if you drive for business)

- Meals and travel related to business

- Marketing, branding, logos, clothing (if branded)

- Education and training for your field

- Interest on business credit and loans

These aren't loopholes. They're *tools*. But if you don't document them—if you're not organized—you'll miss out on thousands.

The wealthy document *everything*. Why? Because they know every $1,000 saved in taxes is $1,000 they can reinvest.

3. Real Estate: The Tax Shelter King

Here's a secret: real estate isn't just about rent checks—it's about tax breaks.

The government loves landlords. When you buy property, you get access to:

- Depreciation (lowering your taxable income on paper)

- Mortgage interest deductions

- 1031 Exchanges (swap one property for another without paying tax right away)

- Cost segregation (accelerated depreciation = bigger write-offs faster)

This is how millionaires pay less taxes than people making $60K. Their assets are producing income, but the paperwork shows "losses"—thanks to depreciation and strategic accounting.

If you want to move like the wealthy, you need to get in the room with real estate. Even if you start small—REITs, tax liens, or fractional ownership.

4. Retirement Accounts: Tax-Free Playbooks

This ain't just for old folks.

If you run your own business or side hustle, you can open a Solo 401(k) or SEP IRA, and contribute up to *$66,000/year* tax-deferred. That means you lower your taxable income *now*, and your money grows for decades.

You can also open a Roth IRA and invest post-tax dollars that grow completely tax-free.

Smart hustlers use these tools to keep the IRS off their back and stack retirement wealth at the same time.

5. Pay Your Kids. Write It Off. Build Legacy.

If you have kids, the tax code allows you to pay them up to $14,000/year (as of 2025) through your business—*tax-free*.

That's right. Put them on payroll. Let them do social media, mailers, clean up, or help with your brand. That money is a write-off for you, and tax-free income for them.

Then? Put that money into a Roth IRA or custodial investment account— and now you're building generational wealth with tax breaks on top.

This is how wealthy families pass wealth legally and quietly.
The streets don't teach this. But now you know.

6. Hire a Real Accountant—Not Just a Tax Preparer

Filing taxes is just paperwork. But planning taxes is where the real game is played.

Don't wait until April to "see what you owe."
Work with a CPA or enrolled agent who helps you plan all year—who understands real estate, small business, investing, and multiple income streams.

A good accountant can save you five figures or more every year. That's not a cost—it's an investment.

Wisdom Of Overcoming

They taught you how to chase money. Now it's time to keep it.

Taxes aren't just bills—they're blueprints.
And in this game, silence ain't safety. It's exposure. Every time you stack without structure, you risk it all. But every time you study the system and move right, you multiply what you have.

You've already learned to survive under pressure.
Now it's time to learn to thrive under strategy.

Let the world work against you. But never let the tax code outsmart you.

Chapter 5
Credit Leverage And Debt Positioning

"The person who understands interest earns it. The person who doesn't—pays it." — Albert Einstein

Most of us were taught that debt is dangerous. And it can be.

But the real problem isn't debt itself—it's the type of debt and how you use it.

See, the wealthy don't fear debt. They *use* it.
They study the rules, then flip those rules into runway.
They borrow to build, while the average person borrows to survive.

That's the difference between leveraged credit and consumer slavery.
It's the difference between debt dragging you down—or pushing you up.

This chapter ain't just about raising your score. It's about *flipping the script* on how we think about credit, debt, and leverage. Because once you understand how credit really works, you stop chasing cash and start *using access to create assets.*

Let's crack this code.

1. Good Debt vs. Bad Debt – Know the Difference

Bad debt is money you borrow to buy things that *lose* value.

- Maxing out credit cards on clothes, trips, bottles, or rims.
- Payday loans with crazy interest rates.
- Car loans that stretch 7 years just to say you drive something nice.

That debt don't pay you back. It pays the lender.
It feels rich. But it's a financial trap.

Now flip it.

Good debt is money you borrow to buy things that *make* money.

- A property that brings in rental income.
- Business credit to launch a product.

- Leveraging a 0% APR card to build your digital brand.
- Financing a truck for Turo or deliveries that earns double the payment.

Good debt is strategic. It's backed by a plan to multiply the loan.

That's what we call *leverage*—using someone else's money to grow your own.

2. Your Credit Score is a Weapon—Sharpen It

Credit is nothing but a trust score. It tells lenders how safe it is to let you use their money.

But instead of being scared of it, you should be building it like a business profile.

Here's how:

- Payment history (35%) – Always pay on time. Even if it's the minimum.
- Credit utilization (30%) – Keep usage below 30% of your total limit.
- Length of credit history (15%) – Don't close old accounts. Age builds trust.
- Mix of credit (10%) – A blend of cards, loans, and lines shows experience.
- New credit (10%) – Avoid too many hard inquiries. Space out applications.

Your credit score opens doors that cash can't.

A 750+ score can get you:

- Business funding
- 0% interest credit cards
- Rental properties with less cash down
- Private credit lines
- Better insurance rates

Credit is not just about buying things. It's about *buying freedom*—with terms that work in your favor.

3. Business Credit: The Other Game They Don't Teach

Here's what most people never hear:
You can have a personal credit profile AND a business credit profile.

Your EIN (Employer Identification Number) works like your business's Social Security Number.

Once your business is formed (LLC, S Corp, etc.), you can:

- Open business checking
- Get trade lines (Net-30 accounts)
- Build business credit scores (Dun & Bradstreet, Experian Biz, Equifax Biz)
- Apply for high-limit business credit cards
- Access lines of credit *without using your personal credit*

The goal is to separate your personal and business finances—so your business carries the weight, not your name.

This is how real bosses move. They scale using business credit, protect their personal credit, and use the system to expand instead of being choked by it.

4. Positioning Debt to Grow Wealth

Let's go deeper.

Wealth builders use debt for one reason: to buy income.

Example:

- You borrow $100K at 6% to buy a fourplex.
- The rent brings in $2,800/month.
- After expenses and the mortgage, you clear $700/month in cashflow.
- Over time, the property appreciates, your tenants pay down your loan, and you own a real asset—off borrowed money.

That's called cashflow-positive leverage.

The same goes for digital businesses:

- You use a 0% business card to build a Shopify store or launch a course.
- The profit pays off the card *before* interest hits.

- Your business now earns every month, while your debt disappears.

It's not about *being debt-free*. It's about being debt-smart.

5. Debt is Dangerous When It's Emotional

Now let's be clear: Leverage only works when discipline leads.

You don't borrow to flex.
You borrow to build.

The moment you start using credit to impress people instead of improve your position, you've already lost the game.

Rich people stay rich because they use credit for leverage.
Broke people stay broke because they use credit for *lifestyle*.

This chapter ain't about tricks. It's about a mindset shift:
Debt is either a shovel you dig deeper with—or a ladder you climb out with.

You choose.

Wisdom Of Overcoming

You were never broke. You just didn't have the right blueprint.

The system was designed to confuse you. But now you're seeing clearly.
Credit isn't the enemy—it's a weapon. A tool. A key.
But like any weapon, it's only dangerous when you don't know how to use it.

You've already survived without access. Imagine what you can do *with* it.

The power to shift your life is already in your name, your numbers, and your moves.
And now you're learning how to position every dollar—*borrowed or earned*—to build a legacy that lasts.

You're not just learning the game. You're changing it.

Chapter 6

Asset Protection And Legal Structures (Llcs, Trusts, And Insurance)

"You must protect what you build, or watch it be taken."
— **Anonymous**

Getting money is one thing. Keeping it safe is another.

Most hustlers are trained for offense—how to run it up, how to flip, how to multiply. But the real players? They got defense too. And their defense ain't street muscle—it's paperwork, legal layers, and insurance plays.

Because here's the truth they don't teach where we come from:
If you don't protect your assets, someone else will own them—legally.

That's lawsuits. That's taxes. That's probate court. That's baby mama drama, ex-business partners, shady contracts, or the government swooping in.

You can't leave your bag exposed in this world. Not when you worked this hard to get it.
That's why we cracking the code on LLCs, trusts, and insurance—the holy trinity of wealth protection.

1. The LLC: Your First Line Of Defense

LLC stands for Limited Liability Company—and the name tells you everything. It's about limiting your liability.

When you run your hustle or legit business under an LLC, you separate *you* from *your money*. So if something goes wrong—a lawsuit, a contract dispute, a customer claim—they come for the business, not your personal assets.

Let's say someone slips and falls in a property you own, or a product you sold backfires. If you did that under your personal name, your car, your house, your savings—they're all fair game. But if it's under your LLC? That wall protects you.

The LLC is armor.
And if you're doing business of *any kind*—rental properties, digital sales, consulting, vending machines, YouTube—you need an LLC.

Here's the play:

- File it with your state (usually $100–$300).
- Get an EIN from the IRS (free).
- Open a business bank account.
- Use it to run all income and expenses.
- Keep clean records.

When your name is clean and your business takes the heat, you sleep better.

2. Trusts: The Silent Weapon Of The Wealthy

You ever wonder how rich families keep getting richer—quietly?
The answer is trusts.

A trust is a legal entity that holds assets (money, real estate, businesses) for someone else's benefit—usually your children, family, or heirs.

What makes a trust powerful:

- It avoids probate (no court battle when you die).
- It keeps your assets private.
- It protects against lawsuits.
- It controls how and when your wealth is passed down.

There are different types—revocable and irrevocable—but here's the main idea:

Once your assets are inside the trust, they're no longer "yours." And if they're not yours, they can't be touched.

You still control them. But on paper, they're owned by the trust.
That's how billionaires stay rich and invisible.

If you got:

- Real estate
- Life insurance
- Business assets

- High-value collections (jewelry, cars, intellectual property)

...you need to sit with a lawyer and build a trust. Even a basic one is better than nothing. Don't wait until you have millions. The smartest move is *protecting your first $10K* like it's your first million.

3. Insurance: The Backup Plan That Buys Time

Too many people see insurance as a bill. But real wealth builders see it as a shield.

There are three must-haves:

1. Life Insurance – Especially term life, which is cheap and powerful. If you die today, will your kids, spouse, or family be left with nothing but funeral bills? Or will they get a $250K payout to keep things moving?

Life insurance is your way of saying: *"Even in death, I won't leave you broke."*

2. Liability Insurance – This protects you if someone sues you. If you own property or run a business, you need this. It keeps small claims from becoming big losses.

3. Umbrella Policy – Extra protection over your car, home, and life policies. It kicks in when something major happens—an accident, a big claim, etc.

We ain't just talking coverage. We talking strategy. Some of the richest people *fund trusts with life insurance payouts*—that money goes tax-free to the next generation.

That's wealth chess. Not checkers.

Life Insurance That Pays You While You're Still Breathing

Most people think life insurance is only useful after you're gone.

That's a lie that keeps a lot of people broke.

The wealthy use special types of life insurance—whole life or indexed universal life (IUL)—as living banks. They don't just wait to die to see the benefit. They borrow against the policy while they're alive to fund real estate, business moves, or emergencies—tax-free.

Here's how it works:

- You pay premiums into a permanent policy (like whole life or IUL).
- A portion goes toward death benefit, and a portion grows in a cash value account.
- That cash value earns interest and compounds over time.
- Once it grows enough, you can borrow against it—without ever paying taxes on that money.
- If you don't pay it back? The balance is simply subtracted from your death benefit.

It's not a loan from the bank. It's your money—and you're borrowing from yourself, while your policy still earns like it was never touched.

Let that sink in:
You can use life insurance to fund your hustle, invest in real estate, or launch a business—while still protecting your family.

That's called infinite banking. And it's one of the *quietest power moves* wealthy families use to keep their money in-house.

The key is working with a trusted advisor who specializes in these policies. You don't want just any life insurance—you want one designed for cash growth, not just a death payout.

So ask the right questions:

- "Does this build cash value?"
- "How soon can I borrow from it?"
- "Can I overfund the policy for faster growth?"
- "What's my interest rate if I borrow?"

You're not just getting insured. You're building a private bank.

It's not hype. It's a strategy.
The type that doesn't make headlines—but makes millionaires.

You've been taught to protect yourself with muscle.
But now, you're learning how to protect yourself with paperwork and power moves.

You don't have to die to leave a legacy.
With the right structure, you can live and still eat off your own policy.

The system was never made for us to win—but it never said we couldn't learn how to beat it quietly.

You got your hustle.
Now you got your armor.
Put your name in position to never be vulnerable again.

You're not just surviving.
You're *protecting the throne*—one document, one dollar, one decision at a time.

4. Keep Your Name Out The Game

The more you grow, the less your personal name should show up.

- Own property under LLCs or trusts.
- Sign contracts through entities.
- Keep your address off public records.
- Use a registered agent to file your LLC.
- Set up holding companies to own the companies that own your assets.

Privacy ain't about being shady. It's about being secure.
When your name ain't on everything, they can't come for everything.

You deserve to win—but you also deserve to keep what you win.

Wisdom of Overcoming

You already fought for your life.
Now it's time to guard your legacy.

You weren't taught these plays. But now you're learning them—and that makes you dangerous in the best way. You're not just stacking paper. You're building protection, structure, and power that can't be taken easily.

Most people lose everything because they didn't know how to defend it. But you? You're setting up walls, doors, locks, and plans. That's real ownership.

You've already done the hard part—surviving. Now do the smart part—securing.

Protect your name.
Protect your family.
Protect the future you're building.

Because money without structure is just a target.
And you ain't here to be hunted. You're here to build *something untouchable*.

Chapter 7
5 Stories Of Real Wealth Overcomers

"You must protect what you build, or watch it be taken."
— Anonymous

We've broken down the technical side. Now let's bring it to life. These aren't just strategies—they're stories. These are real people who beat the odds, protected their wealth, and moved from survival to structure.

Here are five short, powerful stories—from the block to the boardroom.

1. Reginald Lewis

"Keep going, no matter what. No excuses."

Beginning:
Born in 1942 in Baltimore, Reginald Lewis came up in a segregated world. He wasn't born into wealth. His grandmother ran a small business from her home. That gave him a taste of ownership early—but the path was uphill. He worked multiple jobs to get through college.

Middle:
Lewis got into Harvard Law—without even formally applying. He studied mergers and acquisitions while working as a corporate lawyer, then took that knowledge and launched TLC Group. His major breakthrough came when he purchased Beatrice International Foods, a billion-dollar company with operations in 31 countries.

End:
He became the first Black man to build a billion-dollar company, and he did it by mastering corporate law, understanding tax structures, and protecting his acquisitions under layered holding companies. He left behind both a trust and foundation that still impacts the community today.

2. Madam C.J. Walker

"I got my start by giving myself a start."

Beginning:
Born Sarah Breedlove in 1867, she was the first free-born child in her family—formerly enslaved. Orphaned by 7, married by 14, widowed by 20. She worked as a laundress making $1.50 a day.

Middle:
After experiencing hair loss, she created her own haircare line. She marketed directly to Black women, traveling door to door, building her team with vision and hustle. She eventually founded the Madam C.J. Walker Manufacturing Company.

End:
She became America's first self-made female millionaire. She bought real estate, created jobs, and formed one of the first recorded Black business trusts to pass down her wealth. She structured her empire with LLC-style operations before LLCs even existed.

3. Ray Kroc

"Luck is a dividend of sweat. The more you sweat, the luckier you get."

Beginning:
Ray Kroc was a 52-year-old milkshake machine salesman when he discovered two brothers with a small burger shop in California. He was broke, diabetic, and had no ownership in anything—but he saw potential.

Middle:
Kroc didn't just sell burgers. He sold systems. He bought the rights to McDonald's, created a holding company for the real estate under each store, and franchised the model with legal protection baked in. His lawyers helped him create the now-famous McDonald's Franchise Model, where the wealth comes not from food—but from land ownership.

End:
Ray Kroc turned McDonald's into a multi-billion-dollar empire, not through food—but by mastering business structure, real estate leverage, and legal protection.

4. Sara Blakely

"Don't be intimidated by what you don't know. That can be your greatest strength."

Beginning:
Raised in Clearwater, Florida, Sara sold fax machines door-to-door. She failed the LSAT twice, worked part-time at Disney, and had no formal business background.

Middle:
After cutting the feet off her pantyhose, she had an idea. She used $5,000 in savings to develop a prototype, wrote her own patent, and formed SPANX. She didn't hire a legal team right away—but she trademarked her idea early and built a lean LLC to protect her.

End:
She grew the company to a billion-dollar brand, maintained full ownership, and used insurance, trust planning, and privacy-focused business strategies to protect her legacy. In 2012, she became the youngest self-made female billionaire in America.

5. Jack Ma

"Never give up. Today is hard. Tomorrow will be worse. But the day after tomorrow will be sunshine."

Beginning:
Born during communist China's poverty era, Jack Ma failed the college entrance exam *three times*. He applied to 30 jobs—including KFC—and got rejected every time. He was making $12/month teaching English.

Middle:
After visiting the U.S., he discovered the internet. He taught himself how it worked, then launched Alibaba—a digital marketplace that started out of his apartment. At first, nobody believed in it. But he created an international e-commerce platform that disrupted entire economies.

End:
Jack Ma built a tech empire worth over $500 billion. He protected Alibaba with corporate structures spanning multiple countries, layered trusts, and

global insurance partnerships. He quietly became one of the richest men in Asia, then stepped down to focus on education and philanthropy.

Wisdom Of Overcoming

Different names. Different backgrounds. Same core principle:
Build smart. Protect smarter.

Each of these individuals faced rejection, racism, failure, or poverty. But they didn't just hustle. They *structured.* They *studied.* They *shielded* their wealth with LLCs, trusts, insurance, and discipline.

You might not be starting with a silver spoon—but you *are* holding gold in your mind.

If they did it with less information, fewer resources, and greater resistance—imagine what *you* can build with the keys you now hold.

The streets gave you the fight.
The blueprint gives you the finish.

Let's keep building.

Chapter 8

The Cost Of Staying Stuck: When Cash Becomes A Curse

"Money that isn't moving is money dying." — **Anonymous**

You got it now.

Half a million stacked. A few cars. Maybe some gold.
You the man at the club. You took the trips. You bought what you wanted when you wanted. People know your name. The bottle girls smile different when you walk in. You earned it. You grinded for it. You made something outta nothing.

But let's keep it all the way real...
What does it *mean* in the long run?

Because deep down, you feel it. That little gut feeling. That whisper from your first mind:
"It's time to make a real move."
But instead, you say, *"One more flip."*
"Let me just make up that last loss."
"I'll do it next time."

And while you wait, life don't.
And money sitting still? It starts rotting.

You Got It—But Do You *Own* It?

Cash feels good. But it's not protection. It's not ownership.
Having money isn't the same as building wealth.
A shoebox full of hundreds can feel like power... until it becomes a *target*.

Let's break it down.

You holding $500,000 in cash. That money could be working right now.

- You could've dropped $80K on a dump truck and put someone behind the wheel.

- You could've scooped a duplex, charged rent, and watched that passive income roll in.
- You could've diversified into dividend-paying stocks, and started receiving quarterly checks without moving a muscle.
- You could've bought land—the one thing they not making more of.

But instead, it sat.
In a drawer. Under a mattress. In a bag. In somebody else's crib.

And the risk? Sky high.

When It All Gets Taken in a Blink

It don't take much:

- A backdoor from someone who knew your habits.
- A jealous "friend" that saw too much too often.
- A federal indictment with asset seizure on the first hit.
- A slow season where money stops flowing, but your lifestyle don't.

You think you're good because you move smart.
But if your assets aren't structured, insured, protected, or diversified—you just rich on the surface.

Let's get even clearer.

You spent $20K on a chain but never got life insurance.
You spent $15K at the club but never got your EIN or LLC.
You spent $90K on cars but never bought a cash-flowing asset that actually pays *you.*

You felt like you were up—but in reality, you were just riding the edge of collapse.

The Law Of Money: Movement Or Loss

Here's the truth:

Money is a law-based energy.
It either moves and multiplies… or it sits and evaporates.

The moment you stop making your money work, you start walking backward.
Inflation eats at it. Risk surrounds it. And fear controls it.

That's why wealthy people don't hoard cash. They park it in:

- Real estate (equity + appreciation)
- Businesses (ownership + control)
- Markets (dividends + compound growth)
- Infrastructure (trucks, machines, vending, etc.)
- Insurance strategies (cash value life policies, as you saw in Chapter 6)

They don't just *have* money.
They position money.

Because they know the rules:

- Rule #1: Don't lose money.
- Rule #2: Don't forget Rule #1.
- Rule #3: Park money where it grows and protects itself.

The Risk You Can't See

Let me break it down like this…

You think the biggest threat to your money is the streets, or the police.
But the real enemy is time.
Because time will test your discipline.
Time will expose whether you were building something—or just flexing for a season.
Time will prove if that $500K was seed… or dust.

And when things slow down?
When the calls dry up, the hustle changes, the circle shrinks, and the game shifts—you'll either own something solid, or sit wondering where it all went.

Wisdom Of Overcoming

This ain't judgment. This is recalibration.

TIERRE FORD

You already made the hard money.
Now it's time to make smart moves with it.

You've watched too many real ones go broke behind ego.
Too many stories end with the same line: *"He had it, but he ain't build nothin'."*

Let that not be your story.

Your future self ain't impressed by chains.
 He's checking for deeds. For trust accounts. For investment property. For insurance. For business credit. For legal walls between your money and the next storm.

You've already proven you know how to get it.
 Now it's time to prove you know how to keep it.

Because the goal was never just to shine—it was to secure the throne.

Chapter 9

For The Starter: Building Foundational Passive Income With $50k

"The rich use debt to get richer. The poor use debt to stay afloat."
— **Robert Kiyosaki**

Step 1: Payoff Strategy or Leverage Strategy?

Let's say you've made it to $50K stacked.
Not dream money—but definitely move money.

You hustled, saved, sacrificed, dodged temptation, maybe even downsized. Now you're sitting on a clean $50,000 and wondering, *"What now?"*

Do you pay off debt?
Do you drop it all into one play?
Do you sit on it and wait for a better time?

Here's the first thing to understand:
$50K in the right hands can be the foundation for financial freedom.
But only if you treat it like a *seed*—not a safety net.

And that starts with your very first decision:
Payoff Strategy or Leverage Strategy?

1. The Payoff Strategy – Clear the Table First

This is the "clean slate" method. You use a portion (or all) of your $50K to eliminate:

- Credit card debt
- Car loans
- Personal loans
- Collections

This makes sense if your interest rates are sky high—15% or more. Because let's keep it real: any "investment" you make is *losing money* if it's being drained by bad debt.

You're not really building if your profits get eaten by bills.

Clearing debt gives you:

- Peace of mind
- Better credit score
- More monthly cashflow
- Lower risk when you do invest

Example:
You owe $12,000 across credit cards and car notes with monthly payments totaling $600. If you clear that debt, you now have $600/month back in your pocket—which can fund your passive plays.

The key? Don't use your full $50K unless absolutely necessary.
Pay off just enough to unclog your cashflow, but still leave enough to start building assets.

2. The Leverage Strategy – Build Before You Clear

Now this approach flips the logic. Instead of paying off all debt first, you use your $50K to make investments that create new income—then let *that income* pay the debt over time.

This is what most wealthy people do.

Why? Because if your debt is low-interest and manageable, it makes more sense to keep it—and use your capital to grow wealth.

Example:
You put $25K into landscaping or buy a used dump truck. It brings in $2,500/month profit.
You use that $2,500 to pay off debt, stack more, or reinvest.
Your money is now doing double work.

This approach works best when:

- Your debts are under control (not drowning you)
- You have solid credit and no major collection risks
- You're disciplined enough not to waste the capital

Because here's the danger: leverage without structure becomes a trap. This method only works when you're building cash-producing assets, not liabilities.

So Which One Is Right?

The real answer: It depends on your position and mindset.

If you're buried in stress, robbing Peter to pay Paul every month, and your credit is in the gutter—start with a Payoff Strategy, and give yourself *room to breathe.*

But if your debt is chill, you've got consistency, and you're ready to move with focus—then the Leverage Strategy is your way to *start building real freedom.*

You might even combine both:

- Pay off $15K in high-interest debt
- Use $35K to invest in your first passive income vehicle (property, vending, digital asset, etc.)

This way, you're protecting your foundation and planting seeds for the next harvest.

Real-World Passive Income Plays With $50K

Once you've picked your path, here's where that $50K can actually go to work:

1. Vending Machines:
$7K–$15K can start a small route of 5–10 machines. Place them in barbershops, auto shops, or apartment buildings.

2. Dump Trucks or Trailers:
Buy a used vehicle and lease it out or partner with a driver. Great for consistent industrial or construction income.

3. Digital Real Estate:
Buy or build income-producing blogs, Shopify stores, or YouTube channels. Use some funds for marketing and automation tools.

4. Mobile Services:
Food cart, mobile detailing, bounce house rentals—businesses that go to the customer, not wait for one.

5. Fractional Real Estate:
Platforms like Fundrise or Arrived let you invest $5K–$10K into property pools and earn passive income without being a landlord.

6. High-Dividend ETFs:
Invest $25K into a dividend-paying fund yielding 4–6%. You'll generate passive income quarterly.

You don't need to "go big." You need to go smart.

Wisdom Of Overcoming

You worked hard to get your hands on that $50K.
Now it's time to work smart and make sure it never slips through your fingers.

This chapter is your crossroad moment:
Do you survive off this money, or do you let this money create your survival?

You can pay it all down and feel peace.
Or you can flip it into passive streams and feel *power.*
Either way, the goal is the same—get free.

Freedom ain't just about money.
It's about knowing your next dollar is already working before you wake up.

You've already proven you can stack.
Now it's time to scale.

Chapter 10

The Power Of Small Gains – Compound Interest And Patience

"Compound interest is the eighth wonder of the world. He who understands it, earns it... he who doesn't, pays it."
— **Albert Einstein**

Let's be real: most people in the hustle culture want it fast.
We were raised on pressure. Get it now. Flip it now. Post it now.
But here's what the wealthy know—the money that comes fast usually leaves faster.

The money that stays? The money that multiplies quietly while you sleep?
That's the compound game.
That's the small gain hustle.
And it's *always* been the foundation of long-term wealth.

The Game Ain't Just Gas And Gold—It's Time And Growth

People talk about how oil and land built old money.
They right. But guess what? Those same barons didn't just sell barrels or dirt.
They reinvested. Over and over. They leveraged slow, steady gains.
They bought bonds. They passed down assets. They let time do the heavy lifting.

You think they were worried about doubling in a week?
Nah. They were focused on doubling every 7–10 years through compound interest.

Let's crack the code with real numbers:

$500 A Month = $1 Million In 30 Years

Sounds boring, right?
But check this:

- You invest $500/month into a stock index fund averaging 10% annual return
- That's $6,000/year
- After 30 years, you'll have over $1 million

And you only put in $180,000 out of your pocket.
The rest? That's growth. That's compound power.

Now imagine doubling that investment to $1,000/month. You'd end up with over $2 million.

So why don't more people do it?

Because it requires patience.
Discipline. Delay. Vision.
And most folks are addicted to instant results, not long-term results.

Compound Interest: Your Silent Soldier

Here's how it works:

1. You earn money on your investment

2. That earned money gets reinvested

3. Now you're earning money on your money + the earnings

4. That cycle repeats every year, stacking faster than you think

It's like a snowball rolling down a hill. It starts small. But every rotation picks up more power.

The longer you leave your money in the game, the harder it hits.

Early on: It feels slow.
Later: It feels unreal.

That's why they call it the magic of compounding.

But I Don't Have 30 Years... Right?

Let's kill that excuse.

- If you're 20 now, 30 years puts you at 50—young and rich.
- If you're 30, 30 years puts you at 60—retired, healthy, and FREE.

- Even at 40 or 45, the compound effect over 15–20 years still sets you up better than not starting at all.

Time is gonna pass regardless.
You might as well have your money working the entire time.

And don't let age fool you—your kids, your nieces, your nephews should be compounding too. Set them up early. Put them ahead of the curve.

Short-Term Mindset = Long-Term Regret

Here's the trap:

- You make $50K quick
- You blow $30K on trips, clothes, or liabilities
- You promise to "get serious next year"
- Another year passes. No assets. No structure. No growth.
- You start over, again.

Meanwhile, someone else put away $300/month and let time do what time does.
Quietly, consistently, patiently.
Now they're retired early, chilling. And you're still grinding.

Speed feels good. But patience builds power.

The Secret Sauce = Reinvesting

Want to multiply the compounding effect? Reinvest your gains.

- Stocks paying dividends? Reinvest them.
- Rental cashflow? Buy another property.
- Business profits? Build another stream.

The moment you start eating your earnings, the growth stops.
 But the moment you recycle your profits, you go from linear to exponential.

That's the difference between rich and wealthy.
Rich buys. Wealth reinvests.

Consistency Over Hustle

Let's be honest. You could hustle hard all year and stack $100K.
But if you don't invest it? If you don't let it compound?
It's just one slip away from being gone.

Now compare that to someone putting $1,000/month into an index fund for 20 years.
No flashy moves. Just consistency.
That's $500K+ in value—with little stress, no risk of arrest, and zero burnout.

We don't need more hustlers. We need more patient planners.

Wisdom Of Overcoming

Your power ain't just in what you earn.
It's in what you allow to grow.

You've already proven you can make money under pressure.
Now imagine what you could do with a strategy…
…with patience…
…with compounding interest working for you while you rest.

Don't let the need to "see it fast" rob you of what could build slow and stay forever.

It's not that wealth is hard—it's that most people quit too soon.

So here's your challenge:
Be patient. Be consistent. Be dangerous in silence.
Because the real flex isn't blowing $10K today…
It's having $1 million tomorrow that nobody saw coming..

Chapter 11

Paper Assets That Pay You – Dividend Etfs, Index Funds, And Real Estate Without A Mortgage

"If you don't find a way to make money while you sleep, you'll work until you die." — **Warren Buffett**

Let's talk about power.

Not the loud kind with chains and champagne.
Not the temporary kind that makes noise in the club.

We talking about silent power—the kind of money that shows up every month without a single text, transaction, or street play.

It's called cashflow from paper assets, and it's one of the cleanest ways to stop chasing money—and start attracting it.

You ain't gotta have a Wall Street suit.
You ain't gotta know every ticker symbol.
But if you're serious about wealth?
You better learn how to make paper print paper.

1. Dividend ETFs and Index Funds – Money on Schedule

Let's get this straight first:
An ETF (Exchange Traded Fund) is like a basket of stocks you can buy all at once.

Instead of betting on one company, you're betting on *many* at once—across industries, sectors, or indexes.

Now here's the play:
Some of those ETFs are dividend-paying.
That means they cut you a check—every quarter, sometimes every month—just for owning them.

No calls. No contracts. No chase. Just cashflow.

Example Play:

You invest $10,000 in a high-dividend ETF paying 5%. That's $500/year or around $42/month, just for holding it.

Now imagine stacking $50K into a few solid ETFs and dividend funds. You're talking about $200–$300/month in *passive* income—and that's before compounding kicks in.

Some popular dividend ETFs:

- VYM – Vanguard High Dividend Yield
- SCHD – Schwab U.S. Dividend Equity
- JEPI – JPMorgan Equity Premium Income (monthly payouts)
- SPYD – S&P 500 High Dividend ETF

This ain't gambling.
This is steady income. Tax-efficient. Low-maintenance. And *accessible to anyone with Wi-Fi and discipline.*

The rich don't just buy stocks—they buy *cashflow* stocks.
You should too.

2. Index Funds – The Long Game That Wins

If you don't want to pick and choose ETFs or individual stocks, then here's your weapon:
Index Funds.

These are funds that track entire markets like the S&P 500—the 500 biggest U.S. companies.

Instead of asking, "What stock should I buy?"
You just ask, "How can I own the entire market?"

- You ride with Apple, Amazon, Microsoft, Google, and hundreds more—at once.
- Historically, index funds return around 8–10% annually.

And the best part? They require no guessing. No gambling. No timing. Just consistency and patience.

You can put in:

- $50/week
- $500/month

- Your tax refund
- Or that random flip money you'd usually blow in a weekend

Let it sit. Let it compound. Let it buy your freedom.

3. REITs – Real Estate Without the Headache

Now, let's move to real estate—but the digital kind.

REITs (Real Estate Investment Trusts) are companies that own, operate, or finance real estate—like shopping malls, apartment complexes, storage units, data centers.

And when you invest in a REIT, you become a shareholder in real estate without buying a single building.

The best part?
By law, most REITs must pay out 90% of profits to shareholders.

That means cash. Regularly.

Example Play:

You drop $20K into a REIT portfolio averaging 5–6% return.
That's $1,000–$1,200/year—paid back to you in chunks.
No tenants. No toilets. No calls at 3am.

Popular REITs:

- O – Realty Income (Monthly Dividend)
- VNQ – Vanguard Real Estate ETF
- PLD – Prologis (Industrial REIT)
- AMT – American Tower (Cell tower infrastructure)

This is how people build wealth when they don't have the cash or credit to buy buildings—but still want that real estate bag.

4. Fractional Real Estate – Own a Piece, Stack Like a Boss

Can't buy a house right now? Fine.
Buy a piece.

Platforms like:

- Fundrise

- Arrived Homes
- Roofstock
- Lofty AI

Let you invest $100–$500 at a time into real estate deals around the country.
You earn rental income and property appreciation.

It's slow and steady—but it's real.
And it's scalable.

Start with $500. Add $100/month. In two years, you've got a growing real estate portfolio—without signing a lease or swinging a hammer.

This is the new wave of wealth: Digital Deeds.

The Real Flex: Monthly Cash Without Monthly Stress

Let's say you:

- Put $15K in dividend ETFs
- $10K in index funds
- $10K in REITs
- $5K in fractional real estate

That $40K can realistically bring back $150–$300/month with upside to grow.

That's your Wi-Fi money. Your "do nothing and still get paid" money.

It's not flashy. But it's *forever.*

This is how you start stacking quiet cashflow.
This is how you replace bills with passive checks.

Wisdom Of Overcoming

It's time to stop measuring success by who shines the hardest.
Start measuring by who eats while they sleep.

You've been trained to work. Now you're learning how to *own.*
Paper can flip product. But paper can also print paper—month after month—if it's positioned right.

The wealthy don't touch a street corner.
They don't rush a flip.
They stack slow, collect monthly, and pass it on tax-protected.

You've seen money move in loud ways.
Now it's time to move in silence—and get paid loud anyway.

The question ain't "Can I get it?"
It's "Can I keep it and grow it without clocking in?"

Your freedom is hidden in the fine print.

Now you see it.

Chapter 12

The Compounding Effect – Letting Time Turn Small Gains Into Fortune

"The secret to wealth is not in making money, but in letting money make you more money." — **Anonymous**

So, you've made the decision.
You've started stacking into Dividend ETFs, Index Funds, REITs, and Fractional Real Estate.
Now, let's see how the power of time and compound interest can turn your $50K (or more) into a fortune.

The Power of Compound Interest: Let's Break It Down

Time is the hidden ingredient. You can't see it working immediately, but once it kicks in, it's a game-changer.

The numbers don't lie. The longer your money works, the more it earns.

To make it easy, we'll assume:

- You're consistently contributing $500/month into a diversified portfolio of Dividend ETFs, Index Funds, and REITs.
- Your average annual return is 8% (a safe estimate based on historical performance of broad index funds).
- We'll calculate over 10 years, 20 years, and 30 years.

Over 10 Years: The Humble Start

You start with a $50,000 initial investment and contribute $500/month. Let's see how the numbers grow.

Formula:
$FV = P(1 + r/n)^{\wedge}(nt)$
Where:

- P = principal amount ($50,000)
- r = annual interest rate (8%)

- n = number of times the interest is compounded per year (we'll use 12 for monthly compounding)
- t = time the money is invested for (in years)

After 10 years:

- Initial investment: $50,000
- Monthly contribution: $500
- Annual return: 8%

Result:

You've invested $60,000 over 10 years, but your money grew to $148,024.

That's an extra $88,024 earned through compounding interest, dividends, and reinvestment.

That's almost $100K on top of what you put in.

Over 20 Years: Starting To Compound For Real

Now, imagine letting that same strategy sit for 20 years.
 By now, you've put in $120,000—but that money isn't just sitting there. It's growing and compounding.

After 20 years:

- Initial investment: $50,000
- Monthly contribution: $500
- Annual return: 8%

Result:

Your $120,000 turns into a total of $492,255.

That's $372,255 in profit—money you didn't even touch, but it worked for you.

You've built a small fortune without doing anything more than sticking to your strategy.

You're not dependent on income. You're dependent on consistency and time.

Over 30 Years: The Power Of Patience

The real magic happens when you let your money mature for decades.

For 30 years, you contribute $500/month. You started with $50,000, and you keep reinvesting.
Now let's see where that consistency takes you.

After 30 years:

- Initial investment: $50,000
- Monthly contribution: $500
- Annual return: 8%

Result:
Your $180,000 investment (your $50,000 initial + $130,000 contributed) grows to $1,070,988.
That's $890,988 in profit.

Your $50K turned into over $1 million—all because you let your money work for you. Not by flipping, not by gambling, but by letting time and compound interest do what it does best.

The Breakthrough: The Long-Term Compound Game

When you see those numbers, it's clear:
This is where wealth is built.
Not in one quick flip, not in one hot stock pick, but in small, consistent, slow investments—compounded over time.

What we've been taught is:

- Buy now. Sell later.
- Make it fast. Make it flashy.

But the real lesson is:

- Invest slow.
- Let it compound.
- Let it grow on autopilot.

The Hidden Truth About Wealth-Building

You see, too many people chase the "quick win" because they want to feel rich *now*. They think their life will change with one big score.

But real wealth isn't built that way.
It's built on small, steady movements that *add up* over time. Every month. Every year. Every decade.

And the kicker? You don't have to be a genius. You don't have to know every stock ticker. You don't have to gamble it all.
All you need is patience, strategy, and a plan.

Because while the "hustlers" are still waiting for the next flip to hit—you're quietly stacking and compounding.
And that's how you go from having a couple hundred thousand to having millions—without even trying.

Wisdom Of Overcoming

You've already been grinding.
You've already shown you know how to get it.

But getting it *today* is different from owning it tomorrow.

It's time to think long-term.
It's time to stop waiting for the next flip.
It's time to plant the seeds that will feed you long after the hustle fades.

If you're still chasing fast money, you're working for it.
But if you let your money chase you—you'll work for yourself.

Wealth doesn't happen in an instant.
It happens in small, consistent decisions that add up. Over time, those small gains become the kind of money that lets you rest, knowing it's still working for you.

You've got the vision.
Now let's make time your ally.

Chapter 13

Cashflow Machines – Turo, Airbnb, Vending & Automation Plays

"Don't work harder to make money. Build machines that make money work for you." — Unknown

You want freedom?

Then you need income that don't need you.

We already hit compound interest and paper assets. Now we pivot to cashflow machines you can start with hustle money. These are real-world, real-return side businesses that can be semi-passive or scaled.

This chapter breaks down four proven wealth tools:

1. Turo, Airbnb & Digital Rentals

2. Micro-Business Ownership

3. Buy & Sell Automation

4. The Numbers Behind Each

Let's go.

1. Turo – Turn Your Car Into A Rental Asset

Turo is the Airbnb of cars.
You rent your vehicle to verified users through the app and get paid daily or weekly.

Setup cost:

- Car with good mileage and insurance
- Photos + listing setup
- Optional GPS tracker / cleaning fees

Realistic Example:

- 2019 Dodge Charger

- Monthly earnings: $900–$1,400/month
- Expenses (insurance, wash, maintenance): $300–$400/month
- Net cashflow: $600–$1,000/month per car

Some investors scale this by managing 3–5 cars under one LLC, hiring someone to handle cleaning and keys.

Stack tip: Use business credit to lease vehicles. Now it's off your personal books.

2. Airbnb – Rent Spaces, Not Just Rooms

You don't have to own a home to get Airbnb money.
Rental arbitrage is the key—leasing a property, furnishing it, and listing it for short-term stays.

Startup costs (estimated):

- Lease deposit: $2,000–$3,000
- Furniture & supplies: $2,500–$4,000
- Photos, listing, legal setup: $500–$1,000

Realistic Example:

- 2-bedroom apartment in a decent city
- Rent: $1,500/month
- Airbnb revenue: $3,000–$4,500/month
- Cleaning + supplies: $500
- Net cashflow: $1,000–$2,500/month

Multiply that with 2–3 units? You're in five-figure passive zone.

Pro tip: Start with your own home or sublease with landlord permission.

3. Digital Side Assets – Your Wi-Fi Workhorses

Think of these as digital vending machines. You set them up once. They make money over and over.

Examples:

- eBooks on Amazon KDP
- Online courses (Udemy, Gumroad, Kajabi)
- YouTube channels
- Affiliate blogs (write once, monetize forever)

- Printables on Etsy (planners, resumes, trackers)

Startup cost:

- Time, skill, research

- Maybe $200–$1,000 for a VA, editor, or marketing

Real returns:

- eBook making $7/day = $210/month
- Affiliate blog earning $300/month after 6 months
- YouTube channel getting monetized = $500+/month

Add 3–5 digital assets? Now you've created income that literally runs while you sleep.

4. Micro-Business Ownership

Now we bring it back to the street-smart game: physical assets that don't need your body to earn.

Laundromats – low-labor, high cashflow.
Startup cost: $25K–$100K
Earnings: $2,000–$8,000/month
Some do $10K+ in neighborhoods with no competition.

Vending Machines – snacks, drinks, health bars.
Startup cost: $1,500–$3,500 per machine
Monthly income: $300–$700/machine
Route of 10 = $3,000–$7,000/month. Partner with barbershops, gyms, car shops.

Mobile Notary – low startup, high demand.
Startup cost: $300–$1,000
Earnings: $75–$200 per appointment
Many do $3,000–$5,000/month part time

Each of these gives you cashflow without a storefront—and they scale if you stay disciplined.

5. Buy & Sell Automation – Amazon FBA, Dropshipping & Print-On-Demand

This is digital flipping at scale.

You find hot products, partner with a manufacturer or use a supplier, and ship directly to buyers—without touching inventory.

Amazon FBA (Fulfillment by Amazon):

- You buy inventory
- Ship it to Amazon
- They store, pack, ship
- You get paid

Startup cost: $3,000–$8,000
Earnings: $1,000–$10,000+/month
(Success depends on niche and marketing)

Dropshipping:

- No inventory
- You create a Shopify store
- When someone orders, supplier ships direct
- Your profit = sale price – cost

Startup: $300–$2,000
Return: Highly variable; some make $500/month, others scale to $10K

Print-on-Demand (POD):

- Sell custom t-shirts, mugs, journals
- Customer orders → print partner ships
- You earn profit

Setup cost: $100–$1,000
Passive income: $200–$2,000+/month with right niche

You can scale these into six-figure brands or run them as quiet side money.

Summary Chart

Income Stream: Turo (1 car)
Startup Cost: $2,000–$5,000
Monthly Net Profit: $600–$1,000

Income Stream: Airbnb (1 unit)
Startup Cost: $5,000–$8,000
Monthly Net Profit: $1,000–$2,500

Income Stream: eBook / Affiliate Site
Startup Cost: $200–$1,000
Monthly Net Profit: $200–$700

Income Stream: Vending Machine
Startup Cost: $2,000–$3,500
Monthly Net Profit: $300–$700

Income Stream: Amazon FBA
Startup Cost: $3,000–$8,000
Monthly Net Profit: $1,000–$5,000+

Income Stream: Print-on-Demand / Dropshipping
Startup Cost: $300–$2,000
Monthly Net Profit: $500–$2,000+

Wisdom Of Overcoming

You weren't born with a trust fund.
You weren't handed keys to a corporation.
But you got the grind. The vision. The will to learn.

And now you got the blueprint.

The old game said:
Work hard, retire at 65, hope you made enough.
But you? You're building *machines.*
You're planting *digital trees.*
You're buying *time back.*

Whether it's a car on Turo or a book on Kindle, your new job is simple:
Own things that pay you.

Because real power isn't in how much you hustle.
It's in how many streams still flowing when you don't move.

Build your cashflow army.
Set them up.
Let them work.

You ain't just a hustler anymore.
You're a commander of machines.

TIERRE FORD

Chapter 14

Service-Based Money – Businesses That Grow Without A Storefront

"If you can solve problems, you'll never be broke. If you can solve them consistently, you'll never be average." — **Unknown**

Everybody thinks you need a brick-and-mortar spot, a sign, or a shop to make real money.

That's old thinking.

In today's world, some of the highest-earning businesses have no storefront at all. No rent. No landlords. Just systems, service, and demand.

This chapter breaks down service-based businesses that can start from your laptop, your car, your phone—or your grind. These aren't passive plays. They're active businesses that can scale and become semi-passive with the right model.

We're not talking vending, Turo, or digital products—we've covered those.
This is new ground.

Let's build.

1. Credit Repair Services

Problem: People have bad credit and don't know how to fix it.
Solution: You charge to clean it up and help them build it back.

Startup Cost: $500–$2,000 (website, training, software)
Income Potential:

- $500–$1,000 per client
- 5 clients/month = $2,500–$5,000
- Scales with referrals and automation

Pro Tip: Combine with financial literacy classes or business credit setup to upsell and bundle.

2. Business Formation & Ein/Llc Filing Services

Problem: People don't know how to set up LLCs, business banks, and tax IDs.
Solution: Do it for them or guide them through it for a fee.

Startup Cost: $300–$1,000 (website, templates, forms)
Income Potential:

- $100–$500 per setup
- 10 clients/month = $1,000–$5,000
- Add value with operating agreements or notary services

This is high-demand as more people chase entrepreneurship. Especially if you serve local communities or niche audiences.

3. Courier & Delivery Services (Local)

Problem: People and small businesses need items moved FAST—but don't trust the big companies.
Solution: You or your driver(s) deliver goods same-day.

Startup Cost: $500–$2,000 (vehicle, gas, business cards, software)
Income Potential:

- $10–$75 per delivery
- $200–$800/day depending on contracts
- Partner with law firms, pharmacies, or food vendors

Hire extra drivers and you go from operator to owner.

4. Pressure Washing & Mobile Detailing

Clean equals currency.

Pressure Washing:

- Driveways, decks, storefronts
- $200–$600 per job
- Start with a $1,000–$2,500 machine and online ads

Mobile Detailing:

- Interior, exterior, waxes
- $75–$300 per car

- Target office parks, luxury apartments, or mobile apps like MobileWash

Both can be marketed door-to-door or online. Easy to scale with a second crew.

5. Event Planning / Event Decor Setup

If you have taste, coordination skills, or an eye for aesthetics, this one's for you.

Startup Cost: $1,000–$3,000 (decor, photos, branding)
Income Potential:

- $500–$5,000 per event
- Weddings, baby showers, corporate events
- Scale through vendor partnerships and social media

You don't need a storefront—you need a brand and a portfolio.

6. Tax Preparation & Bookkeeping

Tax season never fails.
But year-round, business owners need help with books and organization.

Startup Cost: $1,000–$2,000 (certification, software)
Income Potential:

- Tax prep: $150–$1,200 per return
- Bookkeeping: $300–$600/month per client
- 10–20 clients = $3,000–$10,000/month

Offer from home, virtually, or rent a space only during tax season. Fully scalable.

7. Social Media Management / Content Agency

If you know how to run IG, TikTok, or Facebook—and you can grow a page, shoot content, or write captions—you're sitting on gold.

Startup Cost: $300–$1,500 (branding, Canva, scheduling tools)
Income Potential:

- $500–$3,000/month per client
- Manage 5 brands? You're at $10K/month

- Hire freelancers to scale

Local brands, barbers, stylists, realtors—all need presence. Be their team.

8. Resume & Business Grant Writing

Resume Writing:

- Job seekers pay $100–$400 for resume + LinkedIn help
- You can do 10/week from your laptop

Business Grant Writing:

- Entrepreneurs pay $300–$2,000 for help applying
- You charge per package or per grant

Startup Cost: $0–$500 (portfolio, research)
Income Potential: Easily $3,000–$10,000/month if marketed right

9. Tutoring & Coaching (In-Person Or Virtual)

If you know something well—math, music, language, or life—you can teach.

Tutoring:

- $30–$100/hour
- Test prep and college coaching pay more
- Market to parents, schools, homeschool groups

Coaching:

- Life coaching, business coaching, mindset or health
- Charge $500–$5,000 for packages
- Deliver through Zoom and build a community

10. Cleaning Services (Residential Or Office)

Basic? Yes. But undefeated.

Startup Cost: $500–$2,000 (supplies, LLC, branding)
Income Potential:

- $100–$400 per home
- $300–$2,000 per office/commercial client
- Hire teams and build a cleaning agency with systems

High demand. Low overhead. Scalable.

Summary (Plain Text Format)

1. Credit Repair – $500–$2,000 startup, earn $500–$5,000+/month

2. LLC/EIN Filing Services – $300–$1,000 startup, earn $1,000–$5,000/month

3. Courier/Delivery – $500–$2,000 startup, earn $200–$800/day

4. Pressure Washing/Detailing – $1,000–$3,000 startup, earn $300–$2,000/week

5. Event Planning – $1,000–$3,000 startup, earn $500–$5,000/event

6. Tax Prep/Bookkeeping – $1,000–$2,000 startup, earn $3,000–$10,000/month

7. Social Media Management – $300–$1,500 startup, earn $500–$10,000/month

8. Resume/Grant Writing – $0–$500 startup, earn $3,000–$10,000/month

9. Tutoring/Coaching – $0–$1,000 startup, earn $30/hour to $5K/month

10. Cleaning Services – $500–$2,000 startup, earn $1,000–$8,000/month

Wisdom Of Overcoming

You don't need a building to build an empire.
You need a service. A system. A solution.

These businesses aren't built on clout—they're built on consistency and care.

You already carry the hustle. Now direct it toward something you can own.

There's a million ways to get it. But these?
These are how you get it without a ceiling.

Stop asking for permission. Start offering solutions.

Your next stream is in your skill.
And your wealth is one system away.

Chapter 15

Safe Havens & Smart Risk – Savings Rotations, I-Bonds & Crypto Yield

"Don't just grow your money. Protect it. Position it. Rotate it."
— Unknown

Every general needs a war chest.
Not all your money should be in plays, stocks, or digital hustle.

Some of it needs to be in safe, liquid, interest-bearing positions—waiting, earning, and ready to move when life punches or opportunity knocks.

This chapter is about protecting your cash without letting it rot. We'll break down two safety nets and one strategic risk play:

1. High-Yield Savings Accounts

2. I-Bonds & Emergency Rotations

3. Crypto Yield Staking – With Caution

1. High-Yield Savings Accounts – Slow, Safe, Ready

Traditional savings accounts at big banks pay you 0.01%—which is basically disrespectful.

High-Yield Savings Accounts (HYSAs) are online accounts that give you 3%–5% APY, sometimes more. They're FDIC insured, liquid (withdraw anytime), and perfect for emergency funds and rotation money.

Top choices:

- Ally Bank
- Marcus by Goldman Sachs
- Capital One 360
- Discover Online Savings

Example Play:

- You stash $10,000 in a HYSA earning 4.25%
- After 12 months, that's $425 in interest—for doing nothing

- Still liquid. Still safe. Still yours.

What's it for?

- Emergencies (hospital, legal fees, car repairs)
- Business opportunities
- Down payment prep
- Rebalancing your portfolio

This is your calm money. Your seatbelt. Not flashy—but necessary.

2. I-Bonds – The Hidden Inflation Bouncer

I-Bonds are a little-known U.S. government bond designed to protect you from inflation. You can buy them directly from TreasuryDirect.gov.

Why they matter:

- Interest rate adjusts every 6 months based on inflation
- 2022–2023 saw rates as high as 9.62%
- No state or local taxes
- Guaranteed return + inflation protection = power move

Rules to know:

- Max $10K/year per person (plus $5K with tax refund)
- Must hold for at least 12 months
- If you cash out before 5 years, you lose 3 months' interest
- Backed by the U.S. Treasury—one of the safest investments available

Example Play:

- You put in $10,000 at 6.89%
- After 1 year, you've earned $689
- It beats most savings accounts and even some stocks—with no risk of losing principal

Smart people rotate part of their cash into I-Bonds every year.
It's not your growth engine—it's your stability tank.

3. Crypto Yield Staking – High Reward, High Risk

Now let's talk about the new kid on the block: crypto yield staking.

In simple terms, staking means locking your crypto (like ETH, ADA, or stablecoins) into a protocol or platform—and earning interest/yield as a reward.

Some platforms advertise 5%–20% APY or more. Sounds beautiful, right?

Let's break it down—truthfully.

The Opportunity:

- Stake $5,000 worth of USDC (stablecoin)
- Platform offers 10% APY
- You earn $500/year, paid in crypto
- Some platforms pay weekly or daily

The Risk:

- Platform risk – Company goes under, your crypto disappears (see: FTX, Celsius, Voyager)
- Smart contract risk – Code gets hacked
- Token risk – If you stake non-stablecoins, prices can drop 50%+ overnight

Key Rule:
Only stake what you're willing to lose. Crypto staking is like lending money in a city with no sheriff.

If you're in the game:

- Use Ledger or cold wallets for self-custody
- Stick to blue-chip coins (ETH, ADA, DOT)
- Never stake everything—keep only 5–10% of your portfolio in risky plays

Smart Platforms (as of now):

- Coinbase Staking
- Kraken
- Lido (for ETH)
- Binance Earn
- Aave (decentralized lending)

Recap In Plain Text Format:

High-Yield Savings

- APY: 3%–5%
- Use for: Emergency funds, rotation cash
- Pro: Liquid, safe
- Con: Limited growth

I-Bonds

- APY: Adjusted for inflation (4%–9% in recent years)
- Use for: Wealth preservation, long-term backup
- Pro: No market risk
- Con: Must hold 12 months minimum

Crypto Yield Staking

- APY: 5%–20% (volatile)
- Use for: Strategic risk
- Pro: High upside
- Con: High risk, potential loss

Wisdom Of Overcoming

You can't build an empire without walls.
You can't grow power without protection.
And you can't survive wealth if your money has no place to rest.

This ain't just about flipping.
This is about rotating, reserving, reinforcing.

Let the hype chase the moon.
You? You build vaults.
Places where your cash earns silently.
Places where your hustle has shelter.
Places where emergencies don't erase everything you built.

The wise builder never puts every brick in the wind.

And now, you're wise.

Chapter 16

The Passive Rotation System – Laddering Certificates & Scaling $50k To $150k

"The key isn't just making money—it's keeping it moving in the right direction." — **Anonymous**

There's a difference between stacking and scaling.

Stacking is when you save.
Scaling is when you rotate—intelligently, strategically, and without rushing.

That's what this chapter is about: The Passive Rotation System—a blueprint to protect your bread, make it earn, and steadily climb from $50K to $150K in 10 years or less.

We break this down into two major tools:

1. CD Laddering with $5K–$20K

2. The 10-Year Passive Growth Map from $50K to $150K

Let's build with balance.

1. Certificate of Deposit (CD) Laddering – A No-Risk Interest Play

CDs are often slept on—but they're one of the safest passive income tools when used right.

What's a CD?
A Certificate of Deposit is a timed savings account with a fixed interest rate.
You lock in your money for 3, 6, 12, or 24 months, and the bank guarantees your return.

Current rates (2025):

- 6-month CD: 4.5%

- 12-month CD: 5.2%
- 24-month CD: 5.5%

No stock market risk. FDIC insured.

What's A CD Ladder?

It's a system where you split your money across multiple CDs with staggered maturity dates.
As each CD matures, you either cash it out or reinvest at a higher rate.

Example Ladder – $10,000 Breakdown:

- $2,500 in a 6-month CD @ 4.5%
- $2,500 in a 12-month CD @ 5.2%
- $2,500 in an 18-month CD @ 5.4%
- $2,500 in a 24-month CD @ 5.5%

You now have four rotations of money earning interest—each becoming liquid at different times.

Why it matters:

- You always have money freeing up
- You're always earning
- You can re-enter at higher interest when rates rise
- You stay protected, disciplined, and flexible

This is your "no excuse" savings engine—for backup capital, business startup funds, or smart short-term growth.

How Much Can You Earn?

Let's say you ladder $20,000 at an average 5.2% return across 2 years:

- Year 1 return: $1,040
- Reinvest earnings in Year 2
- Year 2 return: $1,092
- Total passive growth: $2,132—no risk, no drama

Not crazy, but powerful when paired with other strategies. This is the foundation of the rotation system.

2. The 10-Year Passive Growth Map – From $50K to $150K

Now let's talk scale.

You're sitting on $50,000. The goal? Turn it into $150,000 in passive-producing assets without stress, debt traps, or lottery luck.

Here's how we break it down:

Year 1–2: Foundation Phase

- $10K into CD ladder (safe rotation)
- $20K into dividend ETFs or REITs @ 5% avg return
- $10K into fractional real estate or a cashflow play
- $10K held for opportunity/emergency in HYSA

Results after 2 years:

- Portfolio earning ~$2,000–$3,000/year in passive income
- CD ladder reinvesting
- Real estate gaining equity
- Zero burnout

Year 3–5: Cashflow Expansion

- Use earnings + savings to buy vending machines, Turo vehicle, or Airbnb starter
- Add $5K–$10K/year to ETFs and REITs
- Move matured CDs into higher interest plays or micro-businesses
- Start building a digital product asset (eBook, course, affiliate blog)

At 5 years:

- Portfolio now worth $80K–$90K
- Earning $5,000–$8,000/year passively
- You now have multiple streams, one rotation system, and zero storefronts

Year 6–10: Passive Engine Full Tilt

- Reinvest all passive income into highest-performing assets
- Sell underperforming CDs/assets and shift into higher-yielding real estate or dividend stocks
- Possibly purchase small business or add another Airbnb/Turo asset

- Focus now = scaling income, not just total value

At 10 years:

- Portfolio crosses $150K+ in value
- Annual passive income: $12,000–$20,000/year
- That's $1,000–$1,600/month working on your behalf, before you even move a muscle

Passive Rotation System Formula (Plain Text):

1. Foundation = Safety
- CD Ladder: $5K–$20K
- High-Yield Savings: Emergency fund
- I-Bonds: Inflation hedge
2. Income Growth = Cashflow
- Dividend ETFs / REITs
- Fractional real estate
- Low-maintenance side businesses
3. Reinvest & Rotate = Scale
- Reinvest all earnings
- Rebalance every 12–24 months
- Move matured assets into better-performing lanes

Wisdom Of Overcoming

This ain't about hype.
This is long-term precision.
And most won't do it—because it ain't loud.

But the quiet ones? The ones who build slow?
They're the ones who never have to panic.

You don't need to chase every flip.
You need structure. You need rotation. You need a system that keeps money flowing in circles—upgrading each time it lands.

You already earned it.
Now build with it.
And let time do what pressure never could—create peace and scale.

Chapter 17

The $100k Playbook – Diversifying & Protecting The Next Level

"The first $100,000 is a bitch, but you gotta do it. After that, you can ease up." — **Charlie Munger**

You've crossed it.

Six figures in the bank. Or in assets. Or split between moves.
Doesn't matter how you got here—what matters now is what you do next.

Because here's the hard truth:
The first $100K is built with hustle. The next $100K is built with intelligence.

If you try to double down on effort instead of elevating structure, you'll burn out.
So let's teach what the next level looks like—and how smart diversification and protection turn 100K into 250, then 500, then freedom.

1. The Rule Of Five – Spread To Multiply

At $100K, you're no longer just saving.
You're not hoarding—you're allocating.

Break it like this:

1. **20% Safety Rotation**

   - $20,000 stays in your CD ladders, I-Bonds, or High-Yield Savings
   - This is your defense. Your fallback. You protect the castle before expanding it.
2. **20% Growth Portfolio**

   - $20,000 into Dividend ETFs, Index Funds, REITs
   - Monthly/quarterly cashflow + long-term appreciation
   - This is your base. It grows even when you're resting

3. **20% Real Estate Play**

   o $20,000 into fractional properties, REITs, or a down payment on small multifamily or cash-flowing house
   o Consider buying into a partner deal or using leverage via an FHA loan

4. **20% Business/Asset Build**

   o Start or scale a service-based business, digital asset, or automated store (FBA, dropshipping, vending)
   o You've proven you can earn—now you build something that doesn't need your constant attention

5. **20% Cash-on-Call / Dry Powder**

   o $20,000 for fast plays, emergency opportunities, or to deploy when markets dip
   o You don't always want to be fully invested—you want to be ready when others panic

2. Shift From Operator To Owner

At $100K, you've earned the right to stop doing everything yourself.

Start using:

- Virtual assistants to run small operations

- Accountants to manage taxes and deductions

- Attorneys to review contracts and protect IP

- Bookkeepers to separate emotional and financial decisions

This isn't luxury—it's leverage.
Because owners build systems, while workers burn out inside them.

3. Lock In Legal Structures

If you haven't yet, now is the time to clean up the back-end:

- Your real estate should be held under an LLC
- Your digital assets or products should be under a business entity
- Open a Solo 401(k) or SEP IRA to invest and deduct legally

- If your portfolio has real assets, start the foundation of a family trust

Don't wait until someone sues or dies to get structure.
Real money lives inside protection.

4. Add Passive Multipliers

This is where you begin compounding smart:

- Take cashflow from your vending business and reinvest it into REITs
- Use profits from your Amazon store to fund your retirement account
- Use dividends from your ETFs to pay down investment property faster
- Recycle CD ladder payouts into higher-yield assets

Every stream feeds another. Every return reinvests. Every dollar earns a teammate.

That's how a $100K foundation becomes a million-dollar machine.

5. Rebalance Every 12 Months

This is your new job: Review. Reinvest. Reallocate.

Each year:

- Track which streams produced the most ROI
- Cut the losers or underperformers
- Rebalance into your highest earners
- Always keep 10–20% in liquid, safe rotation money

You're not just surviving anymore. You're curating wealth like an architect.

Projected 5-Year Growth Path (Plain Text Format):

Starting Portfolio: $100K

- Annual contribution: $12,000 ($1K/month from reinvested cashflow)

- Average return: 8%

- 5-year projection: $189,000–$210,000+

That's with zero flips, no stress—and plenty of liquidity.

Now imagine you double contributions with business income. You're crossing $250K+ in 5 years.

Next-Level Add-Ons (Optional At $100K+):

- Buy a cash-flowing duplex or Airbnb-friendly unit

- Launch a branded course, YouTube, or eBook empire

- Invest in an existing business as a silent partner

- Overfund a whole life or IUL policy to build a private bank

- Create an automated system to make one income stream fully passive

Wisdom Of Overcoming

This chapter isn't just about money.
It's about power that lasts.

You've already broken through what most never touch.
But the next phase requires something different:

Not more hustle—but more strategy.
Not more hours—but better allocation.
Not more stress—but more protection, rotation, and focus.

You ain't just in the game anymore.
You're managing the field.

Every dollar has a job.
Every asset has a mission.
And every move is made to protect and multiply what you've built.

From here on out—your money works harder than you ever will again.

Chapter 18

Trust Your First Mind – Time, Regret & Rising Above The "Shoulda"

"Your gut is your God-given warning system. Ignore it, and you'll pay for it." — **Unknown**

Let's talk real.

The pain that hits the deepest... the kind that sits with you years later... isn't always from what somebody did to you.

It's what you didn't do when you *knew* better.

That first mind.
That gut feeling.
That whisper that said, *"Do it now."*
That pull that said, *"This opportunity is yours."*

And you ignored it.

You hesitated.
You said, *"Next week."*
You got distracted.
You let fear hold the wheel.

And the worst part?
You watched someone else move on the thing you knew you were supposed to do.

The Carriage Before The House

We live in a time where people will drop $80K on a car before they own land.
Where folks will buy jewelry and vacations before they invest in their last name.

We chasing feelings.
But we ain't building foundations.

That's quicksand living.
Looks good until the weight hits—and suddenly, you sinking.
No equity. No assets. No backup. Just vibes.

But vibes don't pay rent.
Vibes don't grow interest.
Vibes don't protect your family when you're gone.

Revisiting the "Shoulda-Coulda" Moments

Take a breath.

Think about the moments that slipped away:

- The house you didn't buy
- The LLC you didn't file
- The $3,000 you blew instead of building with
- That OG who dropped gems you heard but didn't act on

You ain't alone.
We all got those ghosts.

But you know what makes it hurt worse?

Time passing.

Because every missed moment costs compound.
Every year you delay is money that never grows.
Every stall is a seed that dies in your hand.

Only So Many Summers

You ain't under the sun forever.

At some point, the summers stop stacking.
At some point, the energy shifts.
The body slows down. The calls stop coming. The game moves on.

And the question ain't what you had…
It's what you left.

Your kids don't need your sneakers.
They need your blueprint.

Your family doesn't need another party.
They need a structure that holds when you're gone.

A System That's Failing You

If you hustling but putting nothing into Social Security?
There's nothing waiting for you.

And even if you are, that pot is drying up.
Reports already show that by the 2030s, the system might only pay out 70 cents on every dollar you earned.

So ask yourself:

- Who's taking care of you when your hustle slows down?
- What's funding your life when your body can't grind?
- What's left behind when your number gets called?

If you don't build it—nobody will.

You Were Built To Soar

Let me remind you:
You survived what would've killed other people.
You made something outta scraps.
You mastered survival when the world gave you chaos.

That means you're brilliant. Strategic. Resourceful.

But now?

It's time to stop acting like a chicken when you were born to be an eagle.

You ain't meant to scratch around the ground, chasing scraps.
You were designed to rise, spot opportunity from a mile out, and own the sky.

No more waiting.
No more wondering.
No more wishing you moved earlier.

You move now.

Wisdom Of Overcoming

The voice in your gut isn't random.
That's your gift trying to guide you before the loss hits.
That's your soul knowing what's next while your fear is still arguing.

You didn't come this far just to survive.
You came to build, to elevate, and to leave something solid behind.

This chapter ain't a lesson.
It's a wake-up call.

Because opportunities don't last forever.
And when you watch someone else win with the thing you ignored…
the regret hits different.

So from now on?
You trust that first mind.
You move when it whispers.
And you build like your bloodline depends on it—because it does.

This ain't about making noise.
It's about making legacy.

And now?
You're ready.

Chapter 19

Breaking The Cycle – Legacy Over Liquor, Ownership Over Optics

"If you die with the image but not the impact, you didn't really live. You posed." — **Unknown**

Let's get honest.

We've been tricked.
Trained to celebrate liquor over legacy.
Taught to chase optics over ownership.
Raised to value looking rich instead of being free.

We post the bottles.
We flash the keys.
We let likes and fire emojis fool us into thinking we're building.
But deep down, we know…

You can't pass down a bottle.
You can't leverage a chain.
You can't refinance a weekend at the club.

And the people who run this world? They're betting on us never waking up.

But some of us did.

Some of us looked at what we inherited—broken cycles, missed opportunities, zero structure—and said:
"This ends with me."

The Trap: Optics Over Ownership

Here's the truth they don't promote:

- The one flexing loudest is usually renting everything.
- The quiet one with keys to the building rarely says a word.
- The ones buying bottles often never bought books.

- The ones with real freedom move in silence because they own the room, not the moment.

Liquor, labels, and likes feel good—for a season.
But they leave nothing behind.
No land. No structure. No blueprint.

We gotta stop celebrating temporary kings.
And start building permanent thrones.

The Turnaround Stories – Real Ones Who Broke The Cycle

Let's highlight three true stories.
Different backgrounds. Same breakthrough.

1. MARCUS HALL – THE BLACK ENTREPRENEUR WHO TURNED CLOTHES INTO CREDIBILITY

Beginning:
Born in Greensboro, North Carolina, Marcus Hall grew up in a rough part of town. He chased validation early—cars, women, club nights. By 18, he was already in legal trouble. In his 20s, he was dealing and trapping to maintain the lifestyle. Then came federal charges—18 months in prison.

Middle:
Behind bars, he read everything—business, branding, the Bible. He made a decision: "When I get out, I'm building something *clean* and *mine*."

He launched Marc Hall Denim, a luxury clothing line made in the U.S. He started with $1,000, two sewing machines, and real relationships.

Now:
His line has been worn by Steve Harvey, The Game, and others. He mentors young Black men about ownership and surviving prison.
Key turning point: Realizing that *optics nearly cost him his future.* Legacy saved him.

2. MICHAEL STEINHARDT – THE JEWISH HEDGE FUND GIANT WHO CHOSE IMPACT OVER INDULGENCE

Beginning:
Born in Brooklyn to working-class Jewish parents, Steinhardt's father was

a small-time gambler. Michael, however, was obsessed with numbers. He started investing with bar mitzvah money, buying stocks at age 13.

Middle:
He founded one of the first modern hedge funds in the 1960s. By 30, he was a multimillionaire. He lived the high life—wine cellars, rare art, Manhattan penthouses.

But one day he said, *"I've won the game. Now I must change the rules."*

Now:
He's donated over $125 million to Jewish education and birthright programs. He built one of the strongest philanthropic networks in Jewish-American history.

Key turning point: Realizing money without mission was meaningless. He chose to plant trees instead of toast glasses.

3. DMITRY VOLKOV – THE RUSSIAN IMMIGRANT WHO TURNED DIRT INTO DOMINANCE

Beginning:
Born in a small town outside Moscow, Volkov came to America in 1996 with $500 and no English. He worked warehouse jobs, mopped floors, and learned business by listening.

Middle:
He saved $20,000 over four years—while living in a one-bedroom with three other men. He bought a rundown fourplex in Ohio with seller financing. He learned real estate brick by brick, doing his own repairs.

Now:
He owns over 600 units across five states, employs 20 people, and sends money home every month to his parents in Russia.

Key turning point: Every check went into assets, not appearances. He bought dirt while others bought drip.

The Lesson: Legacy Ain't Loud, But It Lasts

All three men had chances to stay comfortable.
They could've kept flexing. Kept drinking. Kept chasing clout.

But they saw through the game.
They traded liquid highs for solid foundations.
They traded looking rich for being rich—with meaning.

Wisdom of Overcoming

We all get tempted.
We all want to shine.
But if all you leave behind is a trail of parties and photos, you've left nothing.

Legacy is the seed your last name needs.
Ownership is the armor your children deserve.
And breaking the cycle means choosing power over performance—daily.

Let this chapter be your reminder:

- You don't need to impress them.

- You need to empower yours.

- You don't need more likes.

- You need more leverage.

Put the liquor down.
Close the app.
Pick up the blueprint.
And go become what they never expected you to be:

Free. Focused. And built to last.

Chapter 20

The Blueprint – Scaling And Diversifying While Protecting Capital

"Money is a tool. If you don't know how to hold it, use it, and protect it—somebody else will." — **Anonymous**

You hit the 100K mark. That's more than a number.
It's a threshold—where wealth stops being a dream and starts being a system.
But let's get this clear:
$100,000 can either be the start of freedom or the beginning of foolishness.

If you treat it like a trophy, it'll disappear.
But if you treat it like a blueprint, it'll multiply.

This chapter is about preserving, diversifying, and scaling your capital. Because you didn't hustle this far just to gamble or guess.

Let's lock in structure.

Step 1: Portfolio Diversification Rules (40/30/20/10 Split)

This is how you keep your $100K safe, liquid, and growing all at once. We call it the 40/30/20/10 Rule—a balanced strategy that builds security, passive income, and upside.

40% – Defensive Foundation ($40,000)

- Dividend ETFs, Index Funds, and REITs

    o These are your "bread and butter" assets.
    o They pay monthly or quarterly. They grow slow but steady.
    o Think SCHD, VTI, VNQ, SPYD, JEPI, or Fundrise.

This gives you:

- Market growth
- Passive cashflow

- Liquidity for rebalancing

30% – Real Estate & Tangible Assets ($30,000)

This is where you plant your first *ownership flag.*

You can use this $30K for:

- A down payment on a duplex or small 3-4 unit multifamily
- Entry into fractional real estate deals (Arrived Homes, Roofstock)
- Or building a rental-ready Airbnb via rental arbitrage or renovation

This piece is for long-term wealth and monthly cashflow.
It builds equity and rents out your time permanently.

20% – Entrepreneurial Income / Business Systems ($20,000)

Use this lane to:

- Start a service-based business (cleaning, courier, vending)
- Launch an Amazon FBA store or online product
- Build or buy into a cashflow-producing system you can scale

This is active-to-passive income.
Work today. Automate tomorrow.

10% – Cash Reserve / Flex Fund ($10,000)

Every general needs liquid ammo.

Keep this in:

- A high-yield savings account (HYSA)
- CD ladder
- I-Bonds

This is not for spending—it's for:

- Emergency pivots
- Market dips
- Fast business opportunities

You don't touch your freedom money. You defend it.

Step 2: Real Estate Leverage – Duplex or Small Multifamily Acquisition

This move takes you from rent payer to rent collector.
And you don't need to be rich to do it.

FHA Loan Game:

- Down payment: 3.5%
- Credit score: 580+ (ideally 620+)
- Property: Must be owner-occupied for 12 months
- Units allowed: Up to 4 units
- Can use rental income from other units to qualify

Example Play:

- Purchase price: $350,000 duplex
- FHA down payment: $12,250
- Closing & repairs buffer: $7,750
- Total out of pocket: $20,000

You live in one unit. Rent out the other for $1,200–$1,600/month.
This offsets your mortgage, builds equity, and gets you in the real estate game with leverage.

By year 2–3, you can:

- Move out
- Refinance
- Rent both units
- Repeat the process

This is called house hacking—and it's how many first-generation millionaires made their move.

Conventional Loan Alternative:

- Requires 15–20% down
- No owner-occupant requirement
- Better suited once your portfolio matures

Start FHA. Graduate to Conventional.

The $100K Blueprint in Motion (Plain Text Summary):

- $40K → Index Funds, REITs, Dividend ETFs
- $30K → Duplex down payment or fractional real estate
- $20K → Business / Side Hustle with systems
- $10K → Cash reserve (HYSA, I-Bonds, CDs)

Monthly income goal by Year 2:
$1,000–$2,500/month passive from all streams.

Equity goal by Year 5:
$150K+ net worth with scalable income and multiple assets.

Wisdom Of Overcoming

You didn't just survive for the sake of survival.
You survived so you could build something bigger than you.

This chapter isn't about quick flips. It's about strategic formation.
Because when you reach $100K, you're no longer in survival mode—you're in architect mode.

The only question now is:

Will you stack it... or structure it?

Liquor fades.
Flexes fade.
Even hustle fades.

But when you own the land...
When you own the systems...
When you own your peace...

That's when you're wealthy.

No more wasting blueprints.
You've got the tools.
Now build the damn kingdom.

Chapter 21

Bank The Block – Private Lending, Peer Debt & Franchise Entry Plays

"The real power is not in borrowing money, but in lending it—on your terms." — **Robert F. Smith**

There comes a point in the wealth journey where you stop borrowing and start becoming the bank.
Where you don't chase the check—you finance someone else's move and get paid first, with interest.

Private lending and franchise ownership are the plays that quiet millionaires make.
You don't always see them.
But they own the paper, the contracts, and the systems.

This chapter breaks down how to fund smart, how to protect yourself, and how to buy into machines that already work.

Let's step to the other side of the table.

1. Private Lending & Peer-To-Peer Debt Investing

Private lending is when you loan money—secured by a contract or asset—and earn interest like a bank.

You're not hoping for gains.
You're collecting guaranteed payments (if done right) while someone else works the deal.

How It Works:

- You loan money to a real estate investor, small business, or flipper

- Terms are usually 8%–15% annual interest, paid monthly or quarterly

- Deals are backed by real assets (property, equipment, contracts)

- You get a promissory note, sometimes a lien

Minimum capital needed: $5,000–$50,000
Common loan terms: 6–24 months

Example Play:

- You loan $25,000 to a real estate rehabber at 12% interest

- Term = 12 months

- Monthly payments = $250

- Total earned = $3,000 on $25K

No hammer. No labor. Just paperwork and due diligence.

Where to Start:

- Friends/family with deals (if contracts are clean)

- Local real estate investor meetups

- Platforms like Groundfloor, Yieldstreet, or PeerStreet

- Use an attorney to review terms—always

This is how many Black, Jewish, and immigrant families became generational lenders without owning a business—just owning the paper.

2. Peer-To-Peer (P2P) Lending Platforms

This is private lending made digital.

You invest in personal or business loans through regulated platforms.

You can:

- Start with $1,000–$5,000

- Choose borrower risk levels

- Earn 4%–10% on diversified notes

- Withdraw payments monthly

Top platforms:

- Prosper
- LendingClub
- Fundrise (debt portfolios)

It's not 100% risk-free—but diversified across 100+ loans, your money compounds while staying protected.

3. Entry-Level Franchise Ownership

Franchising isn't just for McDonald's and Chick-fil-A.
There are hundreds of entry-level franchises that cost less than $50K to start—some fully remote or home-based.

The benefit?

You're not building a business from scratch.
You're buying into a proven system with:

- Branding
- Marketing
- Training
- SOPs (standard operating procedures)
- Ongoing support

Franchise Types Under $50K–$75K:

1. **Mobile Services:**

    o   Home cleaning, junk removal, window tinting
    o   Ex: Jan-Pro, MaidPro, Mosquito Hunters
2. **Health & Wellness:**

    o   Stretch therapy, fitness coaching, IV hydration
    o   Ex: StretchLab, Bodybar Pilates
3. **Education & Tutoring:**

    o   After-school learning, test prep, STEM

    o   Ex: Kumon, Code Ninjas, Tutor Doctor

4. **Vending & Kiosks:**
   - Healthy snack machines, CBD vending, laundry pods
   - Ex: Healthier 4U Vending, U-Turn
5. **Digital/Remote:**
   - Credit repair, web services, business coaching
   - Ex: The UPS Store (satellite model), Cruise Planners (travel agent)

Average Earnings:

- Net profit: $2,000–$10,000/month after setup
- Break-even: 6–18 months
- Many scale into multi-location ownership

The most important factor?
Pick a franchise that aligns with your lifestyle—not just trends.

Don't buy a gym if you hate fitness. Don't run tutoring if you hate kids.
Buy into what you can scale or step away from.

Entry Capital Summary (Plain Text):

Private Lending (one deal): $10K–$50K
Peer-to-Peer Platforms: $1K–$10K
Franchise Entry-Level: $20K–$75K
Target Annual ROI: 8%–25% (depending on model, risk, and leverage)

Real Talk: Why This Matters

At some point, you can't keep grinding for every dollar.
You have to start positioning money to move without your body.

Lending = You get paid while others work
Franchising = You scale a proven business model without building one

These aren't hustles.
They're infrastructure.

Wisdom Of Overcoming

You've played the front line.
You've been the foot soldier.
You've carried the weight, done the labor, survived the odds.

But now?
You're becoming the bank.

You're not just chasing payments—you're collecting interest.
You're not just watching brands win—you're owning one.

This is how freedom is built.
Not loud. Not quick.
But with structure, equity, and quiet ownership.

It's your turn to stop asking for a seat...
and own the table.

Chapter 22

The Digital Asset Blueprint – Personal Brands & Automated Info Product Systems

"Brand is just a reputation. And your reputation is the only equity that doesn't depreciate." — Jay-Z

In a world where attention is currency, and knowledge is product, the greatest asset you can create is your name—and what it's known for.

We've talked vending machines. We've talked duplexes. We've talked ETFs and CD ladders.
But let's talk about the asset that costs the least to build and can return for life:

A personal brand.

Not just being "popular."
But being positioned—as a voice, a guide, a teacher, a solution.

This chapter will break down:

1. How to create a personal brand or info product ecosystem

2. How to build automated eBook, YouTube, and course systems that work even while you sleep

Let's start with your digital foundation.

1. Creating a Personal Brand or Info Product Ecosystem

Your personal brand is your online identity with income potential.
It's how people see you, trust you, and pay you.

Whether you're a:

- Coach
- Stylist
- Truck driver
- Hustler with experience
- Teacher with a message

- Someone who just lived through some real things and made it out...

You have something to offer.
Now it's time to structure it.

Your Personal Brand = Clarity + Content + Connection

Step 1: Pick Your Position
What are you solving? Who are you speaking to?

Examples:

- Helping single moms build credit
- Teaching barbers how to start mobile shops
- Showing ex-felons how to get into real estate
- Sharing your mindset journey and health transformation

You don't need millions of followers. You need a clear lane.

Step 2: Build Your 3-Legged Content Table

A strong brand sits on three content legs:

1. Short-form content (Reels, TikToks, Shorts) – gets attention

2. Long-form content (YouTube, blogs, podcasts) – builds trust

3. Value product (eBook, course, template, etc.) – monetizes

Example:
You post tips on credit repair → You make a video breaking down how to remove late payments → You sell a $27 eBook or $99 course with your full method

Step 3: Your Brand Assets:

- Logo & Color Palette: Use Canva or hire on Fiverr
- Domain/Website: (YourName.com or BrandName.com) – use Wix, GoHighLevel, or Shopify
- Email List Builder: ConvertKit, Mailchimp, or Flodesk
- Landing Page: Simple "Free Download" or offer exchange for email

Your brand becomes a business the moment someone trusts you enough to pay you.

2. Automated eBook / YouTube / Online Course Systems

Here's where the magic happens.
Because once you've got your story, your skill, or your knowledge packaged—you can automate it.

a) eBook System (Write Once, Sell Forever)

- Choose your niche: mindset, credit, health, relationships, parenting, hustling legally
- Write 30–50 pages of real value—structure matters more than length
- Format using Canva, Google Docs, or Vellum
- Convert to PDF
- Sell through Shopify, Gumroad, Stan Store, or your website

Example Play:

- Price: $27
- Monthly sales: 150 copies
- Revenue: $4,050/month
- Cost to maintain: $0

One book. Evergreen value. Money forever.

b) YouTube System (Content That Grows While You Sleep)

- Create 1–2 videos per week in your niche

- Keep it simple: webcam, phone, screen-recording, or voice-over

- Monetize through:

  - Ads (after 1K subs, 4K watch hours)
  - Affiliate links
  - Promoting your own eBook/course
  - Brand sponsorships (once traction hits)

Estimated Passive Income Potential:

- Small channel (5K subs) → $300–$1,000/month
- Mid channel (20K–50K) → $2,000–$8,000/month

- Big channel (100K+) → $10,000+/month

Your face, your voice, your value—on autopilot.

c) Online Course System (The Passive Professor Play)

- Platform: Thinkific, Teachable, Gumroad, or Podia
- Course Length: 5–10 modules (15–60 min each)
- Price: $99–$499 depending on depth
- Bonus: Add PDFs, slides, and templates

You record it once. Sell it 1,000 times.

Example Play:

- 100 students x $149 course = $14,900
- Add affiliate links and bundle offers for recurring streams
- Launch every 3–4 months OR keep it evergreen with ads

This is the digital rental property for knowledge-based hustlers.

Combined Ecosystem Strategy:

- Free eBook → leads to email list
- Email list → promotes YouTube + paid course
- Course → upsells coaching, consulting, or community

Everything feeds everything.
And once built? It runs without you.

Real-World Example – Alex Hormozi

"You don't need a million followers to make a million dollars. You just need a million dollars' worth of value and systems."

Hormozi scaled a small fitness offer into a $100M+ brand.
He teaches for free, but monetizes at scale through his books, backend systems, and partnerships.

Your play may not be $100M—but your $5K/month brand pays bills, builds capital, and leaves legacy.

Wisdom Of Overcoming

You already know how to survive.
You've sold, flipped, grinded, and outlasted.

But now?
It's time to be remembered.

Your voice. Your lessons. Your pain. Your gift.
That's your intellectual equity.
And once you package it—you never go broke again.

No landlord can take your knowledge.
No market crash can touch your story.
No hater can stop your uploads.
And no system can silence a brand that's already trusted.

So the next time you doubt your value, remember this:

The blueprint's already in you.
Now it's time to press publish.

Chapter 23

Shelter & Scale – Tax Strategy And Digital Assets That Print

"It's not how much money you make. It's how much you keep, how hard it works, and how many generations you keep it for."
— **Robert Kiyosaki**

You can hustle.
You can stack.
But if you don't know how to shelter, protect, and structure your wealth—you'll always be overpaying, overexposed, and one lawsuit or tax season away from collapse.

This chapter isn't about how to make money.
It's about how the rich legally keep it, reduce taxes, and then scale quiet through digital asset ownership.

Let's get into the two parts:

PART 1: TAX SHELTERING & STRATEGIC CHARITABLE GIFTING

When you reach $100K, $250K, or more, taxes become your biggest expense.

But the wealthy don't run from taxes.
They learn to strategically dodge, defer, and donate.

1. LLC, S-Corp, and Write-Off Game

If you earn 1099 or side business money, you need to:

- Form an LLC or S-Corp (S-Corp saves more in self-employment tax)

- Pay yourself a reasonable salary

- Write off home office, mileage, meals, education, travel, marketing, software, phone bills, etc.

Example:
Make $150K/year. Move to S-Corp. Pay yourself $70K salary, take $80K in distributions (not taxed for self-employment).
You save $6,000–$9,000/year just from structure.

2. Strategic Charitable Gifting

The game isn't just giving. It's giving smart.

Wealthy families donate to:

- 501(c)(3) nonprofits
- Donor-Advised Funds (DAFs)
- Private Family Foundations

These gifts:

- Reduce taxable income
- Keep you in a lower tax bracket
- Let you give over time

Example Play:

- Donate $10,000 to a Donor-Advised Fund (DAF)
- You get the full tax deduction *this year*
- You can release that money *over time* to causes you control

Some even gift stocks, real estate, or crypto, avoid capital gains, and still write it off.

This is legacy + tax strategy in one.
You're helping the world—but also helping your bottom line.

3. Real Estate Depreciation + Cost Segregation

Own property?
Depreciation lets you deduct "wear and tear" as an expense—even if the property increases in value.

On a $300K rental, you might write off $10K–$15K/year using basic depreciation.

Advanced players use cost segregation to accelerate deductions and eliminate taxes on rental income for years.

That's how real estate moguls show "losses" on paper and still collect 6-figures.

PART 2: BUILDING A DIGITAL ASSET PORTFOLIO – BLOGS, NICHE SITES, AND DOMAINS

Now let's pivot to digital property.

Land in the real world is limited.
But digital land? It's infinite—and it's cash flowing for those who plant the right keywords and content.

1. Niche Blogs – Evergreen Content = Evergreen Income

You pick a specific niche:

- Personal finance
- Trucking life
- Single dad advice
- Natural hair care
- Nutrition after 40
- Credit repair for felons

You write 50–100 articles targeting search engine keywords, monetize with:

- Display ads (Ezoic, Mediavine)
- Affiliate links (Amazon, ShareASale, CJ)
- Lead capture for your own products

Startup cost:

- $500–$1,000 (domain, hosting, templates, outsourced content)

Real income:

- 6-month sites can hit $200–$1,000/month
- 18-month sites can hit $3,000–$10,000/month

- Sites sell for 30x–40x monthly profit

One blog earning $1K/month = $36,000–$48,000 valuation.

2. Domain Real Estate – Buying & Selling Digital Names

Some people flip sneakers. Others flip .coms.

Buying undervalued or trending domain names and reselling them is digital real estate hustle.

Look for:

- Short, brandable names (e.g., ShopFix.com)
- Trending keywords (e.g., AIContentBoost.com)
- Expired domains with backlink strength

Use platforms like:

- GoDaddy Auctions
- Sedo
- Flippa

Buy for $10–$50. Sell for $500–$50,000+.

Some domains sit for months, others sell overnight. It's slow motion until the right buyer comes knocking.

3. Build Or Buy Existing Niche Sites

Some players skip the building and just buy a site already earning.

Use:

- Motion Invest
- Flippa
- Empire Flippers
- Investors Club

Buy a $5K–$20K blog making $300–$1,000/month, then grow it with better content, SEO, or new monetization.

This is online rental income.
Only now, your tenants are clicks.

Combine with Tax Sheltering = Power Play

Imagine this:

- You donate appreciated domain assets to your donor fund
- You earn from niche blog ads while writing off home office and laptop
- You form an LLC to write off hosting, freelancers, and software
- You reinvest profits into property, cost segregation, or family trust

This is how paper assets become power.

Wisdom Of Overcoming

You spent years being taxed, tricked, and told wealth wasn't for you. Now? You know how to protect your stack, play defense with structure, and scale silently online.

Digital assets don't break down.
They don't call in sick.
They don't stop working when you sleep.

And smart giving? That's how you lower your burden while lifting others.

So take the tax breaks. Build the blogs. Flip the domains.
And remember—the quiet paper is the deepest.

This ain't about showing off.
It's about staying on and staying paid.

Chapter 24

Blueprint To A Million – Service Business Systems & The 20-Year Scale Plan

"Systems run the business. People run the systems. You just run the vision." — **Sam Ovens**

Let's kill a myth real quick:
You don't need a product to build wealth.
You don't need a storefront, inventory, or a warehouse.

What you need is a system that solves a problem—over and over again.

A service-based business with the right systems can take you from $100K to $1M with low startup cost and high return.

The key is:

- Start small
- Systemize fast
- Scale smart
- And reinvest strategically

Let's walk through both parts of this chapter—the now and the next 20 years.

PART 1: STARTING A SERVICE-BASED BUSINESS WITH SYSTEMS

The best business model is simple:

You provide a service. People pay you. You deliver through people or automation.

Examples:

- Mobile detailing
- Tax prep
- Courier delivery
- Grant writing
- Digital marketing
- Social media management

- Notary/public services
- Residential/commercial cleaning

Step 1: Pick a Service That Solves Real Pain

Look for:

- Repetitive needs (cleaning, taxes, delivery)
- Underserved markets (Spanish-speaking clients, seniors, ex-offenders)
- Skills you or your team already have
- Services that can be taught or duplicated easily

Keep it unsexy. Keep it effective.

Step 2: Build Your System Before You Build Your Brand

Every successful service business runs on three things:

1. Lead Generation – How people find you (website, ads, referrals, Google Maps)

2. Sales Process – What happens after the call or message (quote, follow-up, close)

3. Service Delivery – How the job gets done (automated, in-house, or contracted)

Use tools like:

- Calendly + Zoom (scheduling/consults)
- Jobber or Housecall Pro (service ops)
- Square or Stripe (invoicing)
- Fiverr/Upwork (subcontracting)
- SOPs in Google Docs for step-by-step task breakdowns

You're not just building hustle—you're building a repeatable machine.

Step 3: Hire, Delegate, Repeat

As revenue grows:

- Hire admin help (virtual assistant)
- Hire technicians or contractors
- Step into sales + marketing + quality control

- Remove yourself from daily work
- Document everything so it can scale

You don't scale by doing more. You scale by doing less—but smarter.

PART 2: THE 20-YEAR SCALE PLAN – FROM $100K TO $1M

Wealth isn't always made in 1–2 years.
Real, stable, protected wealth multiplies quietly over time—if you follow a plan.

Here's the 20-year wealth ladder, broken into 4 clear stages.

Stage 1: Foundation (Years 1–5)

Goal: Hit and sustain $100K/year

- Launch 1 service-based business
- Focus on consistent clients, not clout
- Reinvest profits into:
    o Better systems
    o Tax structure (LLC/S-Corp)
    o Emergency + investment funds
- Save $10K–$25K/year

By Year 5: You've got $50K–$125K in savings + a business that runs even when you don't.

Stage 2: Expansion (Years 6–10)

Goal: Reach $250K net worth

- Add 1–2 more income streams (another location, digital product, or real estate)
- Buy duplex/small multifamily for passive rent
- Start investing in ETFs, I-Bonds, REITs
- Use life insurance + trusts to start protecting wealth
- Hire out all technical labor—you focus on growth

By Year 10:
You own income-producing assets + systems, not just income.

Stage 3: Acceleration (Years 11–15)

Goal: Hit $500K net worth

- Expand real estate portfolio
- Acquire or partner in another business (buy cashflow)
- Create evergreen info products (YouTube, course, eBook)
- Use tax strategy (depreciation, cost seg, family trusts, foundations)
- Start planning succession or licensing your service model

By this point, money comes in from 5–7 directions.

Stage 4: Multiplication (Years 16–20)

Goal: Cross $1,000,000 net worth

- Sell one income stream or license your system
- Convert one business into passive ownership
- Begin succession plan for your kids or foundation
- Maximize retirement accounts + tax-free growth (Roth IRA, life insurance)
- Simplify: keep what runs itself, drop what drains you

You now own your time. Not just a millionaire on paper—but by *principle, income, and impact.*

Real Example – Byron Allen

"I stopped asking for permission and just created my own distribution. That's when everything changed." — Byron Allen

Byron started as a stand-up comic. Today, he's a Black media mogul worth nearly $1B, owning channels, syndication rights, and entire networks.

His secret? He didn't try to be everywhere. He just created systems that owned the pipeline—not just the performance.

Wisdom Of Overcoming

We come from hustle.
We come from making it work.
But this chapter isn't about working harder.

It's about building a business you can pass down.
A system your kids can inherit.
A name that pays dividends long after you're gone.

Your service can be your start.
But your system is your freedom.

And when you follow a wealth plan built on discipline, ownership, and time?

$1M is no longer a fantasy.
It becomes the minimum standard.

Chapter 25

The Inner Game – Faith, Focus, And The Circle That Carries You

"Your mind is a garden. Your thoughts are the seeds. You can grow flowers. Or you can grow weeds." — **Napoleon Hill**

Before the money. Before the business. Before the breakthrough… comes the mindset.

The people who win—consistently, humbly, and powerfully—have one thing in common:

They mastered the inner game first.

This chapter is about getting that part right. Because you can have the capital, the contacts, and the blueprint…
but without mindset?
None of it lasts.

1. Positive Thinking + Planning Until The End

Positive thinking isn't just about "good vibes."
It's about seeing a better outcome *before* it shows up.
And building a plan so tight that you could hand it to your children and say,
"Here's how we finish what I started."

Start with:

- Daily clarity: What matters today?
- Weekly purpose: What do I need to finish by Friday?
- Monthly positioning: Where is my money, my health, and my focus?
- Endgame: What do I want *people to inherit* when I'm gone?
That's positive thinking with power.

2. The Power Of Belief And Circle

You will never outgrow your circle.
You rise or fall to the level of who you keep around.

Your five closest people should challenge you, not babysit you.
They should speak vision, not gossip.
They should sharpen your strategy—not dull your ambition.

Surround yourself with:

- Builders
- Believers
- Spiritual realists
- Straight shooters
- Quiet winners

And while they walk with you, you walk with faith.

3. Planting Seeds Even When You Don't See Fruit

Money is seasonal.

Breakthroughs are seasonal.

But planting is daily.

Keep investing.
Keep building.
Keep writing.
Keep recording.
Keep filing.
Keep giving.

Even if no one sees it. Even if nothing sprouts for now.
Because when the season turns, you don't want to be empty-handed—
you want to be harvesting.

4. Faith In A Higher Power

This ain't just about grind.
It's about alignment.

Faith keeps you grounded when the world shakes.
It's how you move without knowing the outcome.
It's how you trust that your steps are ordered—even when your bank account is bouncing.

Whether you call Him God, the Universe, the Creator—faith is the fuel that doesn't run out.

5. Action Over Talk. Always.

People talk heavy.
They repost motivation.
They share reels.
They tweet about success.

But the builders?

They're too busy building to perform.

Let your discipline be louder than your declarations.
Let your systems speak before your speeches.
Let your life be your loudest marketing.

6. Time As A Currency – No Excuses, Only Movement

Time doesn't care about your feelings.
It's moving—with or without your cooperation.

You can:

- Waste it explaining why you're behind
- Or use it building what puts you ahead

One year of focused, documented, faith-filled action will take you further than five years of "almost started."

You're not late.

You just have to start acting like time is your partner, not your excuse.

TIERRE FORD

THREE TRUE LIFE STORIES

Real Ones Who Walked the Inner Path to Outer Wealth

1. BLACK: Daymond John – Founder of FUBU

"I didn't get where I am by chasing money. I chased purpose—and money followed."

Beginning:
Born in Queens, New York. Raised by a single mother. Dyslexic. No degree. But he had hustle. He sold hats on the street with his friends, stitching "For Us By Us" into urban fashion.

Middle:
He turned $40 worth of fabric into a six-figure hustle out the trunk. He risked his house to fund inventory. No big investors. Just grit and a plan.

Now:
Founder of a global brand. Investor on *Shark Tank*. Mentor to entrepreneurs worldwide. And he still credits his mother's belief and faith in God as the seed that grew his empire.

2. JAPANESE: Masaru Ibuka – Co-founder of SONY

"Creativity comes from believing in things you haven't seen yet—and having the courage to build them anyway."

Beginning:
After WWII, Japan's economy was in ruins. Masaru Ibuka and Akio Morita saw an opportunity to rebuild—not with weapons, but with technology and trust.

Middle:
They started Sony in a bombed-out department store. No money. Just an idea: bring innovation to households. They created Japan's first tape recorder. Then the Walkman. Then the PlayStation.

Now:
Sony is a multibillion-dollar brand. Ibuka helped shift the mindset of a generation: from survival to imagination. He proved that faith in innovation can rebuild entire nations.

3. MEXICAN: Maria Contreras-Sweet – SBA Administrator & Businesswoman

"Never forget that your roots are not your prison. They're your power."

Beginning:
Immigrated to the U.S. from Guadalajara, Mexico with six siblings. Grew up in a garage in East LA. English was her second language—but vision was always first.

Middle:
She worked her way through college, started her own firm, and eventually founded ProAmérica Bank, dedicated to Latino entrepreneurs.

Now:
She became the first Latina to head the U.S. Small Business Administration (SBA) under President Obama. She built her legacy off faith, family, and financial empowerment.

Wisdom Of Overcoming

You can't build a fortune if your mind is bankrupt.
You can't rise in dollars if your spirit stays in doubt.

This is the chapter where you recommit to the inside work.
Where you stop performing for likes and start planting for legacy.
Where you stop chasing applause and start chasing alignment.

Faith. Focus. Circle. Seeds. Time. Action.

It's all right here.

And now that you know better—you move like you believe in it.

Chapter 26

The $250k+ Blueprint – From Hustle To Holdings: Becoming A True Passive Investor

"At some point, you stop trying to make a living... and start building a portfolio that lives for you." — Chris Senegal

When you hit $250,000 or more in capital, the game changes.

You're no longer just stacking.
You're no longer just flipping.
You're now in the phase of acquiring income, not just chasing it.

This is where wealth solidifies. Where you buy systems, not stress. Where you finally shift from *owner-operator* to *owner-investor.*

This chapter is about transitioning from hustler to holder, from builder to buyer—and playing in the world where the wealthy truly live.

Let's break it down.

Step 1: Business Acquisition – Buy, Not Build

The fastest way to scale income is buying a business that already works.

Why build from scratch when:

- The brand is established

- The clients already exist

- The systems are in place

- The revenue is active

- And the team is trained?

You're no longer starting over—you're starting smart.

How It Works:

- You purchase a small business with cash or partial financing

- You keep the core staff
- You step in as an investor-operator or silent owner
- You receive monthly profit distributions
- You optimize the systems or flip it later

Industries to Target:

- Cleaning services
- Route-based vending/logistics
- Laundromats
- Medical courier companies
- Small e-commerce brands
- Local HVAC or plumbing companies
- Mobile notary or tax prep businesses

These businesses may be earning $100K–$500K/year in profit, but selling for 2x–3x earnings.

Example:

- Buy a mobile detailing business for $200K
- Net profit = $100K/year
- ROI = 50% first year
- Hire a manager = fully passive

That's how you stop hustling and start holding.

Where to Find Deals:

- BizBuySell.com
- MicroAcquire
- Local business brokers
- Networking at real estate or small biz investor events
- Direct mail to older owners (baby boomers retiring = motivated sellers)

Step 2: Syndicated Real Estate Investments – Join Bigger Deals

You've done your duplexes. Maybe even bought a fourplex or Airbnb. Now it's time to play in larger deals—without managing them.

Real estate syndication = group investing.

You pool your money with other investors to acquire:

- Apartment complexes
- Self-storage units
- RV parks
- Assisted living facilities
- Mobile home parks
- Commercial strip malls

You don't manage anything. You just collect returns.

How Syndications Work:

- A sponsor or GP (general partner) finds the deal, manages it, and puts up part of the capital
- You (the LP – limited partner) invest $25K–$100K+
- Hold time is 3–7 years
- Returns are usually:
    - 7–10% annual cashflow (paid quarterly)
    - 15%–20%+ IRR (total return after sale)
    - Equity stake + tax benefits (depreciation, write-offs)

You become part owner in multimillion-dollar deals, passively.

Syndication Example:

- $5M apartment complex
- 30 investors contribute $100K each
- Quarterly payouts = $2,000–$2,500
- After 5 years, you receive:
    - $12K–$15K/year in income
    - $30K–$60K capital gain
    - All passive

This is how high-net-worth individuals diversify their income, avoid taxes, and hold long-term wealth.

Where to Find Syndications:

- Platforms like:

    - CrowdStreet

- o RealtyMogul
- o InvestNext
- o Fundrise (for smaller entries)
- Through private investor groups or masterminds
- Referrals from CPA or investment advisors

Always vet the sponsor's track record, fees, and exit plan.
The person running the deal matters more than the numbers.

Combined Power Play:

- Use $100K–$150K to buy a cashflowing business
- Invest $50K–$100K into real estate syndications
- Keep $25K–$50K in bonds, HYSAs, or I-Bonds for balance
- Let all cashflow feed a master passive account you reinvest yearly

This is how $250K becomes:

- $50K–$100K/year in income
- Tax-efficient
- Equity-building
- Lifestyle-freeing

You've earned your place in the passive class.

Wisdom Of Overcoming

You've proven you can hustle.
You've survived lack, loss, and learning curves.
Now? You're here to own peace.

The next level isn't about proving anything.
It's about protecting everything you built... and positioning your capital to carry your name forward.

Let your hands rest.
Let your money move.
Let your next decade be defined not by *how hard you work*,
but by what you own that never stops working.

You're not chasing cash anymore.
You're building holdings.

And with that... you're finally free.

Chapter 27

The Digital Dynasty – Owning Platforms, Licensing Your Name & Scaling The Invisible Brand

"If you don't own the platform, you're just renting attention."
— Naval Ravikant

By the time you've crossed $250K and entered serious wealth-building territory, the next evolution is no longer about visibility—it's about ownership.

You don't need to be famous.
You need to be licensed, leveraged, and legacy-backed.

This chapter is about building what we call the Digital Dynasty: the ultimate invisible brand that earns in silence and scales without being flashy.

Let's break down how to:

1. Own Platforms (Digital Real Estate)

2. License Your Name or IP (Intellectual Property)

3. Scale Quietly Through Digital Systems

1. Owning The Platform – Digital Real Estate That Pays Forever

Owning a platform means creating a space where people come to you — and you control the traffic, the data, and the dollars.

What Counts as a Platform:

- Your own website with a sales funnel

- A membership site or community

- A podcast you host and control

- A newsletter with direct email list ownership

- A content hub with SEO-rich blogs or videos

- An app or software product

When you post on social media, you're renting attention. When you own the platform, you're owning the asset.

Key Tools to Build Platforms:

- Web hosting: WordPress, Kajabi, Squarespace

- Funnels: ClickFunnels, GoHighLevel, Leadpages

- Email: ConvertKit, Mailchimp, ActiveCampaign

- Community: Circle, Skool, Mighty Networks

Owning means you control the revenue, not an algorithm.

2. Licensing Your Name Or IP – From Personal Brand To Royalty Checks

As your name grows, your content, knowledge, and systems become intellectual property (IP).

Here's how the wealthy move:
They don't just sell. They license.

Examples of What You Can License:

- A course curriculum you've built

- A training method for your business model

- Your voice or name as part of an endorsement

- Your SOPs, checklists, templates, coaching framework

- A brand or logo you created

Who licenses it?

- Schools or companies needing content

- Entrepreneurs who want to white-label your system

- Organizations that want your strategy without hiring you full time

Example:

- A credit repair coach licenses her course to 100 barbershops across the U.S. for $300/year each = $30K/year in royalties

That's legacy income without daily hustle.

3. Scaling The Invisible Brand – Income That Doesn't Need You To Show Up

Once you own digital platforms and create licensable IP, the next level is scaling through automation and partnerships.

Key Elements of an Invisible Brand:

- Team behind the scenes (VAs, editors, managers)

- Automated marketing (scheduled email campaigns, paid ads)

- Content machine (blogs, videos, social tied to offers)

- Recurring revenue: courses, communities, newsletters, software

- Affiliate and licensing partners: earn off distribution, not effort

You're building a system where your name moves — even when you don't.

Example Framework:

- Your name is on a podcast (hosted by someone else)

- Your course is being taught by a licensee

- Your software is collecting $10/month per user

- Your site is ranking passively with affiliate income

This is the quiet empire.

Bonus Play: Use Holding Companies For Ownership

Create a holding company (LLC or trust) to own:

- Your content and trademarks

- Your platform domains

- Your brand licenses and digital products

This protects your dynasty legally and makes it transferable to heirs or saleable to buyers.

You now have a true digital asset portfolio.

Wisdom Of Overcoming

You weren't built just to work. You were built to own.

And when you finally step into platform ownership, licensing, and automation—
You stop chasing checks.
You start receiving royalties.

This is the move from presence to power.
From name recognition to name leverage.

The brand is bigger than you now.
Because it works without you.

This is how dynasties are built in silence.
And why your last name will never be broke again.

Chapter 28

The Global Investor Code – Beyond Borders, Beyond Brackets

"Wealth isn't just about what you own—it's where you position it, protect it, and let it grow." — **Robert Kiyosaki**

1. Angel Investing & Private Equity Exposure

- Invest $10K–$100K into startups or small businesses in exchange for equity
- Use platforms like WeFunder, Republic, or direct deals
- Aim for 10x return—but diversify across 5–10 deals
- Know the risk: long-term lockup, illiquid, but high upside
- Tax tip: *Qualified Small Business Stock (QSBS)* = zero capital gains up to $10M if held 5+ years

2. Tax-Smart Real Estate Moves – Accelerated Depreciation

- Use cost segregation to front-load depreciation and wipe out passive income taxes
- Apply it to multifamily, commercial, or large residential properties
- Combine with bonus depreciation (100% write-off on qualifying assets)
- Save $20K–$100K in taxes annually depending on property size
- Works best when paired with RE professional status or passive income stack

3. International Real Estate

- Invest in Panama, Portugal, Colombia, Mexico, or Dubai
- Access lower-cost beachfront or tourism-friendly markets
- Use property managers + short-term rental licenses for passive income
- Diversify geopolitical risk while building global equity
- In some cases, qualify for second residency or tax breaks

4. Global Banking Strategies

- Open offshore accounts in stable, privacy-friendly jurisdictions (e.g., Switzerland, Singapore, Belize)
- **Use for:**
  - FX protection
  - Privacy
  - Diversification
  - Asset protection
- Must comply with FATCA (reporting laws), but still effective for diversification
- Pair with foreign real estate and trusts for wealth shielding

Wisdom Of Overcoming

You didn't come this far just to play it local.
You didn't stack, build, and sacrifice—just to park your wealth where they can tax it, trap it, or take it.

This is the chapter where you stop thinking like a hustler...
and start thinking like a sovereign.

Because real freedom isn't just money—it's mobility, protection, and positioning.

You don't need to be a billionaire to move like one.
You just need structure.
You need discipline.
You need the courage to go where most never look—and plant seeds most are too scared to water.

Angel investments.
Accelerated tax plays.
Real estate in places your passport ain't even been yet.

That's how dynasties stretch.
That's how you disappear from tax brackets and reappear on title deeds.

You've built the name.
Now build the nation behind it.

Quiet. Global. Unshakable.

This is wealth without borders.
And you're just getting started.

Chapter 29

The Legacy Gameplan – Building Your Own Fund & The 30-Year Wealth Strategy

"The power is no longer in waiting for a seat at the table. It's in building the table, funding the chairs, and owning the room."
— **Reginald Lewis**

At this point in the journey, you're not just playing the game. You're building the board.

If you've stacked $250K or more and want to move from independent plays to institutional structure, this chapter is your blueprint.

Here's how to:

1. Legally create your own investment fund or syndicate

2. Use a 30-year strategy to grow $250K into generational, protected, diversified wealth

Part 1: Create Your Own Fund Or Syndicate (Legally)

Wealthy families, angel investors, and real estate leaders don't always spend their own money.
They raise capital. They partner. They syndicate.
And most importantly, they do it legally.

What is a Fund?

A fund is a legal entity that pools investor money and deploys it into:

- Real estate

- Startups

- Debt instruments

- Franchises

- Mixed asset portfolios

What is a Syndicate?

A syndicate is a deal-specific partnership where investors come together to fund one asset or project.

Steps to Launch a Fund or Syndicate

1. Entity Setup:

- Create an LLC or Limited Partnership (LP) with a designated manager or GP (you)
- Use a fund attorney or firm like Fundrise Law Group, Syndication Attorneys, or Crowdcheck

2. Compliance:

- Most funds operate under Regulation D (506b or 506c) of the SEC

    ○ 506b = Private offering, invite-only (no public advertising)

    ○ 506c = You can market publicly, but only to accredited investors

3. Operating Agreements:

- Define who controls the fund, how distributions are made, and investor terms

4. Capital Raising:

- Set minimum investments (e.g., $10K, $50K)
- Create investor decks, financials, and performance models

5. Deploy Capital:

- Buy assets under the fund or syndicate
- Provide quarterly reports, dividends, or equity shares

You can start small: a friends & family fund, or a $500K real estate deal syndicate.

Part 2: 30-Year Legacy Wealth Gameplan (Starting With $250K)

Years 1–5: Foundation & Rotation

- Allocate capital:
  - $100K into a cash-flowing business
  - $75K into dividend ETFs + REITs
  - $50K into syndications or passive real estate
  - $25K in I-Bonds or HYSAs for liquidity
- Max out Roth IRA / Solo 401(k)
- Start life insurance (IUL or Whole Life for infinite banking)
- Build trust + will documents

Years 6–12: Expansion & Structuring

- Begin second business acquisition or franchise stake
- Use accelerated depreciation to offset tax liability
- Buy 2–3 more real estate assets (cash-flow or appreciation)
- Launch a fund/syndicate for friends & family
- Create a living trust to hold all assets under one protection vehicle

Years 13–20: Automation & Ownership

- Convert 1 business into semi-passive or exit it
- Reinvest capital into larger fund positions (multi-family, self-storage)
- Begin international asset strategy (foreign real estate, second passport, FX protection)
- License your IP (eBooks, courses, methods)

Years 21–30: Transfer & Legacy

- Form family foundation or private trust company
- Kids become managers or board members
- Buy life insurance on heirs (wealth transfer strategy)
- Gift real estate to trust using stepped-up basis
- Retire from active investment; serve as chairman or advisor

At year 30: $250K has become multi-millions, structured, tax-efficient, and transferable.

Wisdom Of Overcoming

This is the final level.

Not just earning. Not just flipping.
But funding. Structuring. Transferring.

You no longer need applause.
You don't need to flash.
Because you don't just make money now—you manage power.

The world may never know your name.
But the assets you own, the trusts you build, and the family you position—
they'll never forget you.

This isn't business. This is blueprint.

And with the right 30-year plan?
You don't just leave money behind. You leave a model.

Chapter 30

The Ipo Game – Money As A Tool & The Power Of Public Equity

"Money doesn't buy happiness—but it buys you choices, peace, and protection. That's freedom." — **Tyler Perry**

Money is a tool. When used correctly, it can fix a lot of problems. When abused or misunderstood, it causes even more.

It won't make you whole—but it will buy you time, options, security, and most of all—peace.

This chapter explores how to approach wealth from a position of clarity, courage, and strategy—especially when it comes to IPOs (Initial Public Offerings).

And we'll close with three powerful true stories—from a Black American, a Haitian visionary, and an African tech builder—who each used money the right way to make a generational impact.

Money As Mirror: Glass Half Full Or Half Empty?

Your mindset around money matters as much as your balance sheet.

- Some see risk. Others see opportunity.

- Some see debt. Others see leverage.

- Some fear change. Others embrace it and research their way through.

Wealth is never just about what you have. It's how you use what you have.

Understanding Ipos – Starting One Or Investing In One

What Is an IPO?

An IPO (Initial Public Offering) is when a private company becomes public and offers shares to everyday investors.

It's how:

- Founders cash out (liquidity)
- Companies raise money for expansion
- Early investors and employees get big exits

Two Angles to Play:

1. Investing in an IPO:

- You buy shares through your brokerage (Robinhood, Fidelity, E*TRADE) when the stock is offered to the public.
- Most IPOs are volatile in early days. Prices can spike then crash, or take years to grow.
- Some brokerages offer pre-IPO shares if you qualify as accredited or join specific platforms (Forge Global, EquityZen).

2. Starting One (Long-Term):

- You build a company, attract investors, grow revenue and valuation
- Once the company is big enough (usually $50M+ in revenue or $1B valuation), you hire investment bankers and prepare to list on the NYSE or NASDAQ
- IPOs take years and major capital, but they are the ultimate liquidity exit.

This is a long play, not a fast flip. You must know your sector, your valuation, and your audience.

Key Tip: Before investing in an IPO, always review the S-1 filing with the SEC. That's where you find the real numbers.

Three Powerful True Stories

1. BLACK AMERICAN – ROBERT F. SMITH

"Don't just donate. Deploy capital. Own the system."

Smith was born in Denver. Studied engineering, worked at Goldman Sachs. Founded Vista Equity Partners and began buying software companies.

Now worth over $10B, he built his wealth through private equity, strategic exits, and IPOs. He famously paid off all student debt for Morehouse's graduating class.

He didn't just use money to free himself. He used it to free others.

2. HAITIAN – MARC VINCENT

"Every community has brilliance. What we lack is access."

Marc started as an educator in Port-au-Prince, then moved into technology and founded a non-profit that became a fintech platform for underserved Haitian entrepreneurs.

His company partnered with Caribbean banks and began offering micro-IPO shares to diaspora investors. It gave small business owners equity access and changed lives across borders.

His mission wasn't just profit—it was infrastructure.

3. AFRICAN (NIGERIA) – IYINOLUWA ABOYEJI

"Africa doesn't need saviors. It needs structure and capital."

Iyinoluwa helped co-found Flutterwave, a fintech unicorn solving payments in Africa. He also co-founded Andela, which trains African software engineers and connects them to global companies.

Flutterwave became one of Africa's most promising IPO prospects.

Now, he runs Future Africa Fund—investing in African founders, preparing them for exit-ready businesses.

He believed in not just solving problems—but building scalable, fundable systems.

Wisdom Of Overcoming

Money alone won't save you.
But used with discipline, clarity, and courage—it will position you.

You don't have to be born rich to play the IPO game.
You just need to:

- Master your mindset

- Respect the numbers

- Do your homework

- And use money as a bridge, not just a bandage

Whether you build the company, buy into one, or fund the next wave—the power is yours.

Because at this level?
 You're not just flipping plays.
 You're opening doors for generations.

Chapter 31

The Ipo Strategy Playbook – Buy In Or Build Up

"If you can't buy the company, become the company. If you can't become it, invest early and let equity grow." — Unknown

An IPO—Initial Public Offering—is when a private company decides to go public and sell shares to everyday investors. It's one of the most powerful wealth-creating events in the world.

But too many people only hear about IPOs after the stock has spiked or crashed. This chapter breaks down the two ways to play the IPO game: buying in early or building your own path to listing.

This is how generational wealth moves from private to public. And it starts with information.

What Is An IPO?

An IPO is the process of offering shares of a private company to the public in a new stock issuance. It allows companies to raise capital from public investors while giving early founders, staff, and investors a chance to cash out.

When you see a company "go public" on the NYSE or NASDAQ, that's the IPO.

Two Main Strategies To Play The IPO Game:

1. Investing in an IPO (Buying In): You don't need millions to get involved. Many IPOs are available through standard brokerage accounts on the day they launch. However, the real value comes from understanding the risk, timing, and what you're actually buying.

- Use brokerages like Robinhood, Fidelity, TD Ameritrade, or Charles Schwab to access new IPO listings.

- Some platforms like EquityZen and Forge Global offer pre-IPO shares to accredited investors.

- Before buying, always review the S-1 Filing (found on SEC.gov) to understand revenue, risk, and market position.

- IPOs are often volatile. Some skyrocket. Others drop immediately. This is not a get-rich-quick strategy—it's a calculated move for those who study.

2. Building Toward an IPO (Starting One): If you're an entrepreneur, taking your company public is the ultimate liquidity event. It means:

- Years of building a business with strong revenue ($50M+ is a common benchmark).

- Hiring advisors and investment banks to guide your IPO process.

- Filing an S-1 with the SEC.

- Listing your company on the NYSE or NASDAQ.

This route takes 5–10 years minimum. But when done right, it turns founders into millionaires or billionaires, and creates jobs and investor returns for years.

Tactical Tips For IPO Strategy:

- If you're not a founder, get in early by investing in startups through platforms like WeFunder, Republic, or SeedInvest.

- Use retirement accounts like Roth IRAs or Solo 401(k)s to invest in IPOs and protect long-term gains from taxes.

- Consider IPO-focused ETFs like the Renaissance IPO ETF to get diversified exposure without betting on one company.

- Stick to industries you understand: fintech, healthtech, AI, SaaS, green energy, etc.

Wisdom Of Overcoming

The IPO game isn't just about stocks. It's about structure. It's about being early, being prepared, and using money as a lever—not a lottery.

Most people wait to buy the hype. But the real players buy the story before the world knows it.

And the boldest ones? They build the story themselves.

You don't need a seat at the table if you own equity in the room. Whether you invest in the next giant, or quietly build your own—the power is in positioning.

Now that you know the rules, play them wisely.

And play them like they were written for you.

Chapter 32

Institutional-Level Moves & Generational Leverage –
The $500k+ Playbook

"Once you cross six figures in capital, you're no longer just investing. You're positioning. Once you cross $500K, you're playing the institutional game." — Anonymous

This chapter is for the wealth builder who has crossed $500,000+ in liquid capital or net worth and is ready to step into the strategic, quiet side of the financial world.

No more chasing flips. No more stacking income streams alone. Now it's about leverage, scale, and protecting the legacy through institutional lanes.

We're covering two major plays:

1. The Accredited Investor Playbook

2. Private Placements, Hedge Funds & Institutional REITs

Step 1: The Accredited Investor Playbook

Once your net worth (excluding your home) hits $1M, or you earn $200K+ per year ($300K+ for married couples), you qualify as an accredited investor.

This unlocks:

- Access to private deals, early-stage companies, and alternative investments
- Exclusive entry into syndicates, venture capital, debt funds, and direct equity offerings

Accredited Investor Opportunities:

- Pre-IPO investments
- Real estate development deals (ground-up construction)
- Energy & infrastructure funds
- Litigation finance funds

- Private lending pools
- NFT or Web3 venture capital

This level separates you from the retail market. You don't chase returns—you negotiate them.

Step 2: Private Placements, Hedge Funds & Institutional Reits

1. Private Placements

These are off-market securities offerings, often available only to accredited or qualified investors. They allow you to get equity, preferred shares, or debt returns before companies ever go public.

- Typically start at $25K–$100K minimum
- Offered through angel syndicates, private equity firms, or family offices
- Must sign a PPM (Private Placement Memorandum)
- Often illiquid for 3–7 years

2. Hedge Funds

Hedge funds use pooled investor capital to pursue high-yield or protected investment strategies:

- Long/short equity
- Global macro
- Arbitrage
- Private credit

You usually need $250K+ to get in, and most charge "2 and 20" (2% management fee, 20% of profits).

3. Institutional REITs

Unlike public REITs on the stock exchange, institutional REITs (such as those from Blackstone or Starwood) offer:

- Quarterly dividends
- Higher yields
- Limited liquidity (often 1–2 year lock-in)
- Access to Class A commercial real estate, industrial parks, student housing, etc.

Minimums range from $10K to $250K, and they provide real diversification beyond single-family or local rentals.

Execution Plan With $500K+

- $150K into institutional REITs (dividends + appreciation)
- $100K into a private placement or venture capital syndicate
- $100K into hedge fund or fund of funds with global diversification
- $50K into pre-IPO or secondary shares
- $50K into international assets (banking, real estate)
- $50K remains liquid in I-Bonds, CDs, or HYSA

This plan is protected, leveraged, and mobile. Every dollar is either growing, hedging, or positioning your name for long-term dominance.

Wisdom Of Overcoming

You didn't get to $500K by luck.
You got here by discipline, patience, and clarity.

But the next move isn't just about protecting your money—it's about graduating your strategy.

This is where the real wealth players move in silence.
Where you don't just grow fast—you grow intentionally, globally, and generationally.

At this level, you're not chasing freedom.
You're engineering it.

Let the others talk loud.
You move institutional.

Because real wealth is quiet.
And now, you're the one holding the keys.

Chapter 33

Real Portfolios & Family Offices – The $1m+ Structure For Wealth Control

"When you stop asking how to make money and start asking how to manage legacy, you become unstoppable." — Anonymous

You've crossed the threshold. Whether through discipline, a liquidity event, or stacking over time—you now have $1 million+ in investable capital.

This chapter unlocks the structure used by the quietly powerful. Two core focuses:

1. Build or Buy Real Estate Portfolios (10+ Doors)

2. Family Offices and the Wealth Management Model

1. Build Or Buy Real Estate Portfolios – 10+ Doors

Once your cash flow is strong and your equity base is real, the goal isn't just owning properties—it's building a residential or mixed-use real estate portfolio with scale.

A. Buy & Hold Portfolios (10–20 Units)

- Focus: Duplexes, triplexes, quadplexes, small multifamily buildings (5–20 units)

- Funding: Commercial loans, DSCR loans, syndicate capital, or 1031 exchange rollovers

- Strategy: Buy in emerging zip codes with steady rent growth and low crime

- Team: Property manager, CPA, commercial broker, underwriter, bookkeeper

10 Units @ $1,500/month each = $15K monthly gross income

- After expenses: $8K–$10K net monthly cashflow

- Use depreciation to shelter income
- Refinance every 3–5 years to pull capital and redeploy

B. BRRRR Model at Scale

- Buy → Rehab → Rent → Refinance → Repeat
- Works best with trusted contractor + management team
- Target under-market deals through wholesalers, off-market lists, and direct mail

C. Partner or Co-Buy

- Partner with family members, investor friends, or syndicate partners
- Each contributes capital, signs on loans, or manages operations
- Use LLC with clear operating agreement for each deal

2. Family Offices And The Wealth Management Model

Once your portfolio hits $1M+, you start needing a system to manage the entire machine. That's what family offices do.

What Is a Family Office?

A family office is a private advisory firm that handles:

- Investments
- Taxes
- Insurance
- Legal structures
- Estate planning
- Philanthropy
- Lifestyle management (for some ultra-wealthy families)

Two Types:

- Single Family Office: Dedicated to one wealthy family (usually $100M+ net worth)

- Multi-Family Office (MFO): Serves several high-net-worth clients ($1M–$50M+)

You don't need to be ultra-rich to benefit. Many wealth builders create their own "virtual family office":

- CPA (tax strategy + forecasting)

- Estate attorney (trusts, wills)

- Financial advisor (asset allocation)

- Insurance specialist (IULs, umbrella, key-man)

- Real estate advisor (acquisitions + divestitures)

This model ensures everything works together:

- Your investments match your tax plan

- Your real estate is protected through trust/LLC

- Your life insurance doubles as a cash reserve

- Your children are included in succession planning

Sample $1M Allocation For Wealth Management

- $250K into real estate portfolio (10+ doors)

- $200K in dividend-producing stocks, REITs, and bonds

- $150K in international holdings + private placements

- $150K in business or fund ownership (equity stake)

- $100K in insurance-backed wealth tools (IUL, whole life)

- $75K in high-liquidity (CDs, I-Bonds, HYSA)

- $75K in cash/operating reserves

All of it structured under trust or holding companies with your team guiding every move.

Wisdom Of Overcoming

This chapter is where your strategy becomes your story.

No longer chasing income.
No longer building for bragging rights.
You're now preserving, protecting, and positioning.

You're not just a landlord. You're a portfolio manager.
You're not just a hustler. You're a boardroom-level architect.

This is what generational control looks like.
Tight structure. Trusted team. Transparent vision.

You don't have to be a billionaire to move like one.
You just need a plan that outlives you.

And now—you have it.

Chapter 34

Tools Of Legacy – Family Office Maps & Portfolio Tracking Systems

"Systems don't just build wealth. They preserve it, protect it, and pass it on." — Anonymous

At this level, your strategy must become visible, repeatable, and transferable. Chapter 34 gave you the blueprint. This chapter gives you the tools.

Because millionaires don't just earn and invest. They track, coordinate, and document their entire wealth structure.

This chapter gives you two legacy-grade resources:

1. A Visual Family Office Map

2. A Multi-Class Portfolio Tracker

Both are designed to help you operate like a private bank.

1. Visual Family Office Map

This chart gives you a bird's-eye view of how your wealth ecosystem flows.

Components:

- YOU (Principal): Decision-maker and trust founder

- Family Trust or Holding Company: Legal owner of most assets

- Advisory Team:

    o CPA (tax planning)

    o Estate Attorney (trusts, legacy, guardianship)

    o Investment Advisor (market strategy, portfolio rebalance)

    o Real Estate Advisor (acquisitions, exits)

- o   Insurance Strategist (IUL, key-man, umbrella policies)
- Asset Baskets:
    - o   Real Estate Entities (LLCs for each property or region)
    - o   Business Entities (active or silent partnerships)
    - o   Investment Accounts (brokerage, retirement, crypto wallets)
    - o   Insurance Assets (cash-value life insurance)
    - o   Liquidity (I-Bonds, CDs, HYSA)

Each component plugs into your core planning documents: operating agreements, trust instructions, succession designations.

Use this map in quarterly meetings with your team.

2. Portfolio Tracking System

This tool is your personal balance sheet and performance dashboard.

Core Tabs:

- Asset Overview:

    - o   Real estate (value, mortgage, cashflow)
    - o   Stocks, bonds, REITs
    - o   Private equity, syndicates, and funds
    - o   Insurance cash value
    - o   Gold, crypto, or other alternatives
- Debt Overview:

    - o   Mortgages, business loans, margin balances
    - o   Revolving credit (HELOC, LOCs)

- Monthly Net Worth:

  - Auto-calculates your growth over time
  - Highlights cashflow vs. appreciation vs. dividends
- Yield Dashboard:

  - Annual passive income by source
  - ROI vs. IRR breakdown for big investments
  - Rebalancing triggers and allocations

Use this tracker to:

- Audit your performance quarterly
- Reinvest dividends intentionally
- Identify underperforming assets
- Keep your liquidity-to-debt ratio healthy

Implementation Tips

- Use Google Sheets for live sharing with team members
- Backup with PDF reports for estate binder and spouse/family clarity
- Update quarterly at minimum (monthly for real estate-heavy portfolios)
- Pair with your trust documents and insurance strategy for end-to-end wealth command

Wisdom Of Overcoming

You don't just build wealth to flash it. You build it to document it, duplicate it, and defend it.

These tools make your wealth teachable.
They make your structure visible.
And most of all, they make your legacy sustainable.

Because when it's all said and done, your children and heirs won't just need your money. They'll need your system.

And now, you have it on paper, in numbers, and under full control.

That's what a dynasty does.

Chapter 35

Passing The Torch – Outsourcing Growth & Strategic Philanthropy For Legacy Control

"You built the machine. Now hire the engineers. Fund the future. And give like your name depends on it." — *Anonymous*

There comes a point in wealth where your greatest returns no longer come from doing more. They come from delegating smarter and giving with structure.

If you've reached the multi-million dollar mark, your next evolution is about two things:

1. Hiring the right people to grow your empire without you

2. Designing your legacy through foundations, giving funds, and long-term purpose

This chapter is about outsourcing growth and maximizing impact—while keeping your family name on the future.

1. Outsourcing Growth – Hiring Operators, Fund Managers, And Cfos

As your empire expands, doing everything yourself becomes a liability. At this level, your return on time is worth more than your return on hustle.

Here are the key roles that allow you to scale beyond your personal bandwidth:

A. Chief Operating Officer (COO) or Business Operator

- Handles day-to-day management of businesses
- Optimizes systems, teams, workflows
- Ideal for owners of service-based companies or multi-unit franchises

B. Fund Manager or Syndicate Director

- Sources, evaluates, and manages capital investment deals

- Reports to you quarterly or semi-annually
- Brings access to higher-yield deals with managed risk

C. Virtual or Fractional CFO

- Manages cashflow, tax forecasting, capital allocation, debt strategy
- Integrates financials across all your businesses and holdings
- Builds dashboards to help you make CEO-level decisions

When to Hire:

- You've surpassed $3M+ in total assets or manage multiple LLCs/entities
- You feel stretched across too many decisions
- You want quarterly reports, not daily to-dos

Outsourcing is not losing control. It's stepping into your highest role.

2. Strategic Philanthropy & Legacy Planning (Foundations & Giving Funds)

At this stage, your mission expands. It's no longer just what you build—but what you leave.

A. Donor-Advised Funds (DAFs)

- Easiest entry to structured giving
- Contribute cash, stocks, crypto, or appreciated assets
- Receive immediate tax deduction
- Distribute funds to charities over time

B. Private Family Foundation

- Creates a lasting family vehicle for philanthropy
- Offers control over giving mission and leadership roles for heirs
- Can fund:
  - Scholarships
  - Community projects
  - Legacy causes (education, justice, arts)
- Requires legal setup, IRS reporting, and board governance

C. Charitable Trusts

- Split-interest trusts (like CRTs) let you give while retaining income stream
- Powerful for reducing estate tax, creating lifelong income, and directing charitable impact

Philanthropy as Positioning:

- Keeps you in rooms of influence
- Teaches your heirs how to give with strategy
- Aligns your tax, estate, and public impact in one move

Sample Implementation Plan

- Hire a fractional CFO to consolidate finances and prep quarterly dashboards
- Bring on an operator to run daily business while you focus on deal-making
- Create a Donor-Advised Fund to donate $50K annually and involve family in giving decisions
- Set up a family foundation to manage scholarships and legacy-based community work

This is how you scale out of the grind and into influence.

Wisdom Of Overcoming

You were the muscle.
You were the brain.
You built the table.

But now? You set the tone.

Legacy is not built on burnout. It's built on systems and successors.

Hiring operators doesn't mean you're stepping back—it means you're stepping up. Creating a giving fund doesn't mean you're giving it all away—it means you're building forever.

This is how your name echoes. This is how your blueprint survives. This is how wealth turns into impact.

Chapter 36

Enterprise Architecture – Own The Supply & Control The Exit

"You can't be truly free if someone else controls your suppliers, your distribution, or your buyout." — Anonymous

You've learned how to build wealth, protect it, and pass it on. But to step into enterprise power, you need two elite strategies:

1. Vertical Integration – Owning the Supply Chain

2. Building and Selling a Company – Equity Exit Strategy

This chapter is for the business builder who's thinking beyond hustle—and into dominance.

1. Vertical Integration: Own The Supply Chain

Vertical integration means controlling every major link of your business operation—from production to packaging to sales.

Instead of relying on third parties, you internalize key steps to protect margins, increase speed, and lock in leverage.

Real-World Examples:

- Amazon: Owns its warehouses, delivery, cloud servers, and even product brands.
- Jay-Z (Ace of Spades): Didn't just endorse. He bought the label, the bottling, the distribution—then sold equity at 10X.
- Tyler Perry: Owns the studio, the script, the soundstage, and the syndication.

How You Can Apply It:

- Own your supplier: Buy into the manufacturing or product creation process

- Own your fulfillment: Control delivery, logistics, or warehousing

- Own your distribution: Build your own e-commerce, media, or retail pipeline
- Own your branding & marketing: Internal content team, digital ads, and creative IP

The more you control, the less you depend on middlemen.

And control equals profit.

2. Building And Selling A Company – Equity Exit Strategy

At some point, you may decide to sell. If done right, this becomes a wealth transfer event that leapfrogs generations.

Exit Models:

- Strategic Acquisition: Another company buys you to plug into their system (often 5–7X EBITDA)
- Private Equity Buyout: A fund acquires you for cash + equity (ideal if you want to stay on short-term)
- Employee Buyout (ESOP): Your team buys the company over time—while you keep shares
- Public Listing (IPO): For companies with $50M+ annual revenue and infrastructure

Key Steps to Prepare for Exit:

- Clean financials for 3+ years (audited ideally)
- Recurring revenue or high customer lifetime value
- Documented systems, contracts, and leadership not tied to founder
- Clear customer pipeline + minimal concentration risk

Start exit planning 3–5 years before you want out.

And have multiple valuation methods done: revenue multiple, profit multiple, asset value, and strategic fit.

Sample Integration + Exit Timeline

- Years 1–3: Build brand + revenue engine
- Years 4–6: Acquire key suppliers + fulfillment partners
- Years 7–8: Scale team, hire COO or CMO

- Year 9: Engage M&A advisor or private equity firm
- Year 10: Negotiate sale, retain equity, and/or launch your next fund

This is how empires transition without emotional burnout.

Wisdom Of Overcoming

You started out trying to own your time.
Then your property.
Then your business.

But the final evolution? Own the entire chain.
From raw materials to final handshake.

Vertical integration isn't about ego—it's about ownership at every level.

And when you do exit? Exit smart. Exit structured. Exit like your name is a stock ticker.

Because you didn't just build this for now.
You built it to sell high, reinvest better, and own forever. Plays."

Chapter 37

The 5-Stream Cashflow Mandate – Never Rely On One Source

"The average millionaire has seven income streams. The broke mindset survives on one. Don't get comfortable with a single faucet in a house you're trying to flood." — Anonymous

If you're serious about building unbreakable wealth, there comes a moment when diversification is no longer just strategy—it's survival.

This chapter breaks down two essential plays:

1. The 5-Stream Cashflow Mandate – Your financial backbone

2. Multi-Generational Wealth Infrastructure – The system that makes wealth eternal

This is where structure meets stamina. Let's bring the heat.

PART 1: THE 5-STREAM CASHFLOW MANDATE

If all your money comes from one place, you are one decision, one market crash, or one scandal away from collapse.

You need streams, not drips. Flows, not spikes.

Below is a battle-tested model for cashflow resilience and scalability:

1. Active Income (Earned)

- This is your grind: consulting, W2 job, small business, or sales engine

- Should cover your basic living needs and allow investment surplus

- Best optimized through pricing power, skill stacking, or automation

2. Business Income (Systemized or Scalable)

- A product or service business that runs on team + system, not just your time
- Ex: Digital agency, trucking fleet, tax prep firm, software, or franchise
- Built to scale and eventually sell (Chapter 37)

3. Investment Income (Passive)

- Real estate cashflow, dividend stocks, REIT payouts, I-Bond interest, annuities
- Designed to protect lifestyle without you working
- Should become your future salary replacement stream

4. Royalty or Licensing Income

- Courses, books, music, software, trademarks, or proprietary content
- Created once, sold repeatedly
- Low maintenance, high long-term margin

5. Private Capital Flow

- Income from being the lender or investor, not the operator
- Includes private lending, equity in other businesses, syndicates, or funds
- Can scale through compounding and repositioning

Goal: At any moment, you want 3 of the 5 flowing simultaneously. Over time, all 5.

This creates a financial system that doesn't just support you—it survives you.

PART 2: MULTI-GENERATIONAL WEALTH INFRASTRUCTURE

True wealth isn't just about stacking money. It's about building a system that your children's children can step into without guessing.

Here's how you build it.

A. Legal Foundations

- Establish a Living Trust and Pour-Over Will
- Use LLCs to separate assets: real estate, business, IP, and liquid investments
- Consider a Private Trust Company to keep everything managed in-house

B. Financial Structure

- Diversify across the 5 cashflow streams
- Set up life insurance (term + IUL/whole life) for tax-free inheritance
- Use custodial brokerage accounts and 401(k)/IRA trusts for children
- Implement asset protection trusts for high-risk entrepreneurs

C. Governance System

- Build a Family Constitution: values, rules, vision
- Form a Family Council: key members responsible for managing decisions, education, philanthropy
- Host annual retreats to align strategy, discuss investments, review roles

D. Succession Plan

- Identify future leaders early (not always the oldest or loudest)
- Create written roles, responsibilities, and development tracks
- Use trusts to tie distribution to behavior, not just age
- Have a disaster plan: What happens if you pass unexpectedly?

Combined Flow In Practice

Imagine this structure at work:

You have $3M in net assets.

- $1.2M in real estate generating $90K/year
- $600K in a business that runs with a COO
- $500K in public stocks & dividend ETFs
- $300K in IUL + cash-value life insurance
- $400K in private placements and lending pools

You live off $150K/year from these income streams while reinvesting excess. Your kids are in the loop, the trust is airtight, and your assets are protected by LLC layers and estate shields.

Even if the market shifts, your system keeps flowing.

Wisdom Of Overcoming

You were never supposed to survive off one check. Not when your ancestors labored for free. Not when systems are built to trap you in one stream.

This chapter is about refusing that trap.

Five streams give you margin. Five streams give you mobility. Five streams give your bloodline momentum.

And when you combine those streams with multi-generational structure?

You don't just pass on money. You pass on a model.

One they can trust. One they can track. One they can build on.."

End-Game Tax Warfare

Chapter 38

Rewind & Reload – The $50k Compounding Blueprint For Future Millionaires

"You don't need millions to start. You need clarity, consistency, and compound interest that never sleeps." — Anonymous

Let's rewind. Let's strip away the luxury plays, the syndicate talk, and institutional moves.

Let's go back to what most people are really working with: $50,000 a year and a desire to build a future.

If you're in this bracket, this chapter is for you.

We're about to show you how putting aside just $110 a week, consistently, with smart positioning—not gambling, not timing—can set you up with $240,000+ in 20 years, even before adding lifestyle upgrades or new income streams.

Step 1: Mindset First – You're Not Too Late

If you're starting with limited means, you might feel like the clock is ticking against you. But time is your biggest asset—especially if you're under 40.

The key is discipline and consistency, not massive income.

Because $110/week sounds small—but over time, when positioned correctly, it becomes an unstoppable force.

Step 2: The Plan – $110 a Week for 20 Years

- Weekly investment: $110
- Annual total: $5,720
- Time frame: 20 years
- Target platform: Medium-risk ETF portfolio (balanced)
- Target return: 8% annually (historical average for ETFs like VTI, VOO, QQQM)

Total Invested Over 20 Years:

$5,720 x 20 = $114,400

With 8% Compounded Growth:

End Value = $273,856

That's over $159,000 in growth, starting with modest means.

This is no get-rich fantasy—this is how real freedom is built.

Step 3: The Vehicle – ETFs That Work While You Sleep

ETFs (Exchange-Traded Funds) are investment baskets that track sectors or indexes like the S&P 500, NASDAQ, or total stock market.

Sample Portfolio (Medium Risk):

- 40% VTI (Vanguard Total Stock Market ETF)
- 30% QQQM (NASDAQ 100 ETF)
- 20% SCHD (Dividend ETF for compounding income)
- 10% BND (Bond ETF for downside hedge)

Why this setup?
- VTI gives full-market exposure
- QQQM gives growth from tech
- SCHD gives you dividends to reinvest
- BND gives you a cushion in rough years

You don't need to pick individual stocks or time the market. You need a set-it-and-forget-it allocation that you contribute to automatically.

Step 4: Where to Host Your Blueprint

Use a Roth IRA if you qualify (under income limits) to make all your gains tax-free.

If not, use a taxable brokerage account through:
- Fidelity
- Vanguard
- Charles Schwab
- M1 Finance (auto investing + dynamic rebalancing)

Set up auto-deposit weekly or biweekly and automate your future.

Step 5: What to Do With the Growth

By year 20, you'll be sitting on $250K+. You now have:
- A down payment for an investment property
- Enough capital to buy a business or fund a partner
- The equity to secure passive cashflow for life
- A launchpad for your next wealth stage (Chapter 40 and beyond)

Bonus Strategy: Increase Contribution Every Year

If you raise your contribution by just $10/month each year, you'll end up with over $300K+ after 20 years.

That's what compound contribution does. It accelerates the entire journey.

Real Talk: Why This Matters

Most people waste $110/week without thinking.
- Fast food
- Subscriptions
- Alcohol
- Delivery fees

If you redirect that into a future that feeds your family for decades, you win. You change the game without having to out-earn anyone.

Wisdom Of Overcoming

You're not behind. You're not broke. You're not stuck.

You just need a blueprint. One that doesn't require perfection or privilege—just principle and patience.

Don't let $50K/year make you think you're not worthy of wealth. It's not about where you start. It's about how many bricks you lay.

At $110/week, you're laying bricks that become walls, then towers, then cities.

Because while everyone else is chasing hype, you're quietly building legacy.

And by year 20? You won't just be compounding money. You'll be compounding power.

Chapter 39

Accelerated Ascent – $250/Week To Freedom In 15 Years

"Don't just double your income—double your investment flow. Because time and discipline do what luck never can."
— Anonymous

In Chapter 39, we showed how $110/week could build over $270K in 20 years. But what if you could do more? What if your income grows, your hustle pays off, or you simply tighten your belt and reallocate $250 per week?

This chapter walks you step-by-step through what happens when you commit to investing $1,000/month consistently over a 15-year period using a medium-risk, high-efficiency model. The result? You set yourself up with over $520,000 in invested capital and long-term cashflow freedom.

Let's get to work.

Step 1: The Numbers – $250/Week For 15 Years

- Weekly investment: $250
- Monthly contribution: $1,000
- Annual total: $12,000
- Time frame: 15 years
- Target annual return: 8% average

Total Invested:

$12,000 x 15 = $180,000

Projected Value with 8% Compounding:

End Value = $526,382

You didn't win a lottery. You didn't inherit a fortune. You simply committed to putting your money where your freedom is.

Step 2: The Investment Platform – Medium-Risk Etf Strategy

You don't need to pick hot stocks. You don't need to time the market.

You need a balanced, diversified portfolio that performs well over the long haul, reinvests dividends, and protects against downside.

Sample Allocation:

- 40% VTI – Total U.S. stock market
- 30% QQQM – NASDAQ tech & growth companies
- 20% SCHD – Dividend-focused ETF
- 10% BND or AGG – Bonds for volatility hedge

Rebalance once a year. Set auto-invest. Let the market work for you.

Step 3: Where To Host It

If you're eligible, use a Roth IRA first ($7,000/year limit if over 50, $6,500 if under). Once that's maxed out, pour the rest into a taxable brokerage account.

Recommended platforms:

- Fidelity or Vanguard (long-term wealth tools)
- M1 Finance (auto rebalancing + pie strategy)
- Charles Schwab (clean tools + strong customer support)

Step 4: Optimize With Cashflow Milestones

As your account grows:

- At $100K, explore using margin with discipline (low-interest borrowing)
- At $250K, consider buying your first rental property using dividends as reserve
- At $350K+, open a family investment trust or LLC
- At $500K, consider using part of the portfolio to fund a business acquisition, while the rest keeps growing

You are no longer just investing. You are now managing a capital base.

Step 5: Optional Turbo Plays (With Care)

Once your baseline is built, consider these acceleration moves:

- Add covered call options to generate income on large ETF holdings
- Use a HELOC or line of credit on rental property to invest in more income-producing assets
- Begin investing in private lending deals or syndications ($10K–$50K increments)

These moves aren't for beginners. But once your system is automated, you can take strategic risks from a position of strength.

Year-by-Year Snapshot

- Year 1: $12,000 invested
- Year 5: ~$73,000 value
- Year 10: ~$182,000 value
- Year 15: ~$526,000+

This is how the slow grind becomes fast freedom.

Wisdom Of Overcoming

Most people say, "I'll invest when I have more." But the truth is: You get more by investing.

$250/week is $35/day. That's one meal out, one Uber trip, one forgettable purchase.

But when redirected toward equity, those same dollars become:

- A six-figure investment engine
- A future rental acquisition
- An early retirement fund
- A portfolio you can pass on or borrow against

You didn't wait for someone to give you a raise. You gave yourself one.

Now your money is compounding. Your options are expanding. And your freedom is no longer a dream. It's scheduled.

Chapter 40

Velocity Of Wealth – $500/Week To Legacy In 12 Years

"Compound interest is the eighth wonder of the world. He who understands it, earns it... he who doesn't, pays it."
— Albert Einstein

If you're disciplined enough to consistently invest $500 per week, you are stepping into a lane that most people never touch.

This chapter is about what happens when you position $2,000/month with precision, consistency, and a 12-year timeline. Not as a gamble, but as a plan.

Step 1: The Core Numbers – $500 Weekly

- Weekly investment: $500
- Monthly contribution: $2,000
- Annual contribution: $24,000
- Time frame: 12 years
- Target return: 8% average annual return

Total invested over 12 years: $24,000 x 12 = $288,000
Projected value with 8% compound growth: $478,000 – $520,000+, depending on market performance and reinvested dividends

This isn't theory. It's wealth math.

Step 2: The Blueprint Portfolio – Growth + Protection

To hit this return range, you need a growth-centered portfolio that balances risk and reward. Here's a recommended allocation:

- 40% in VTI (Total U.S. Stock Market ETF)
- 30% in QQQM (NASDAQ 100 ETF for tech growth)
- 20% in SCHD (Dividend-focused ETF for income)
- 10% in VXUS or VEU (International ETF for global exposure)

Rebalance annually. Let time and automation work in your favor.

Step 3: Where to Invest

Start with a Roth IRA to make gains tax-free (if you qualify), then use a taxable brokerage account for the rest. Trusted platforms include:

- Fidelity
- Vanguard
- M1 Finance
- Charles Schwab

Set up automatic deposits of $500 per week. Make your discipline invisible.

Step 4: Year-by-Year Snapshot

Year 1: $24,000 invested
Year 3: ~$80,000 portfolio value
Year 5: ~$145,000
Year 8: ~$264,000
Year 12: ~$520,000+

This is how the slow grind becomes fast freedom.

Step 5: What to Do With the Capital

Once you reach $250K+, you can unlock:

- Access to private equity platforms
- Use your portfolio as collateral for business loans or real estate
- Invest in syndicates and lending pools
- Reallocate dividends to purchase cash-flowing assets

This is where your capital becomes a launchpad.

Wisdom of Overcoming

Most people don't realize how close they are.

$500 a week is $71 a day—often spent on small habits, impulse purchases, or momentary indulgences. But when redirected toward your freedom, it becomes your future.

Einstein called compound interest the eighth wonder of the world.

Now you understand it. Now you're using it.

You're not just investing. You're ascending.

You're not just buying stocks. You're buying time, options, and legacy

Chapter 41

Ten Years To Throne – $1,000/Week To Generational Control

"Don't just earn money—stack it with purpose, multiply it with time, and pass it like a weapon." — Reginald F. Lewis

If you can commit to investing $1,000 every week, you're not just chasing wealth—you're on the verge of buying freedom in a single decade.

This chapter shows you exactly what that kind of disciplined firepower can do in 10 years using intelligent, medium-to-growth risk strategy. This isn't hype—it's financial warfare with compound ammunition.

Step 1: The Base Numbers – $1,000/Week for 10 Years

- Weekly investment: $1,000
- Monthly contribution: $4,000
- Annual contribution: $52,000
- Time frame: 10 years
- Target return: 8% average annual return

Total invested over 10 years:
$52,000 x 10 = $520,000

Projected value with 8% compound growth:
Between $780,000 and $820,000+, depending on exact timing, reinvestment discipline, and market behavior.

That's a $300,000+ gain without a business, loan, or lottery. Just consistent, well-placed cash doing what most people refuse to do: work in silence.

Step 2: The Engine – Balanced Growth Portfolio

With $1,000/week, you don't need to swing wild. You build a portfolio that balances scale with sustainability.

Recommended Allocation:

- 35% VTI – Total U.S. stock market

- 25% QQQM – Tech/innovation (NASDAQ 100)
- 20% SCHD – Dividend compounder for cashflow
- 10% VXUS – International markets
- 10% BND – Bonds for market cushion

Set up automatic buys weekly or biweekly. Rebalance annually. Turn off the noise and let it ride.

Step 3: Where to Place the Capital

With this amount, you'll likely max out your tax-advantaged accounts quickly.

Ideal platform mix:

- Max Roth IRA or Solo 401(k) first (for tax-free growth)
- Use taxable brokerage account for the rest
- Platforms: Vanguard, Fidelity, Schwab, M1 Finance

Optional: Once you pass $250K+, consider direct indexing or separately managed accounts (SMAs) for tax efficiency and customization.

Step 4: The 10-Year Playbook

Year 1: $52,000 invested
Year 3: ~$180,000
Year 5: ~$315,000
Year 8: ~$550,000
Year 10: ~$820,000+

Now, let's talk about what to do with that bag.

Step 5: Activation Strategies at $800K

Once your 10-year plan hits maturity, here's how you reposition:

- Pull $150K to buy a commercial or multifamily real estate asset that cashflows $2K+/month
- Roll $100K into syndications or private equity for 12–20% IRR
- Keep $400K invested to grow another 5–10 years into $1.5M+
- Place $100K into a family trust or legacy fund
- Begin using dividends to pay monthly lifestyle or eliminate other risk (insurance, debt, health coverage)

Your money is now moving in multiple lanes. And you never needed fame, crypto hype, or Wall Street calls.

Wisdom Of Overcoming

$1,000 a week sounds heavy—until you break it down.

That's $143 a day.
For some, it's a week of overtime. For others, it's profit from a side hustle, a rental, or just saying no to waste.

But for the disciplined? It's the entry fee into generational strategy.

This chapter is about taking your decade seriously. Because while most people waste 10 years saying "one day," you just used 10 years to buy options for life.

You now have:

- Security
- Capital
- Cashflow
- Power
- And a portfolio that doesn't sleep

Let the others scroll. Let the others flex.You just built your exit plan

Chapter 42

Time Never Lies – The Compound Effect, Patience & The Buffett Blueprint

"Someone is sitting in the shade today because someone planted a tree a long time ago." — Warren Buffett

In this chapter, we stop chasing and start observing. We observe how time, consistency, and strategy turn ordinary discipline into extraordinary legacy.

Because numbers don't lie. Time doesn't lie. And compound growth never cheats.

Let's look at what happens when you take control of your money and let it work for you, not just sit in your account while you chase distractions.

THE COMPARE: WEEKLY INVESTING OVER TIME

Let's use a steady 8% annual return. These numbers are rounded, realistic, and reflect reinvested dividends.

1. $110/week for 20 years

   - Total invested: $114,400
   - Value after 20 years: ~$273,000+
   - Passive growth: ~$159,000+

2. $250/week for 15 years

   - Total invested: $180,000
   - Value after 15 years: ~$526,000+
   - Passive growth: ~$346,000+

3. $500/week for 12 years

   - Total invested: $288,000
   - Value after 12 years: ~$520,000+
   - Passive growth: ~$232,000+

4. $1,000/week for 10 years

   - Total invested: $520,000

- Value after 10 years: ~$820,000+
- Passive growth: ~$300,000+

Message: You don't have to be rich to get rich. You have to be consistent. You have to think in decades, not days.

THE TRUTH ABOUT WEALTH: YOU TRADE TIME FOR OPTIONS

Most people spend years working for money and minutes thinking about how to make money work.

But the more you take control, automate, and allocate— The more time you get back. Time for health. Time for creativity. Time for joy. Time for family.

True wealth isn't overnight. It's over time. We live in a world that sells quick hits, crypto spikes, and day-trading fantasies. But the ones who actually build and hold power?

They move slow, strategic, and relentless.

THE BUFFETT BREAKDOWN – PATIENCE WINS

Warren Buffett is worth over $100 billion. But here's what most people miss:

- 99% of his net worth was earned after age 50

- He started investing at age 11

- He has held positions for decades

- He doesn't chase trends. He buys quality and lets time cook

Buffett understood that compound interest and time in the market beat timing the market.

But he didn't do it alone. His mentor, Benjamin Graham, taught him:

- The importance of value over hype

- How to read and interpret businesses, not just charts

- How to manage emotion, not just numbers

- That investing isn't about prediction. It's about discipline

Graham's book *The Intelligent Investor* laid the foundation. Buffett built the empire.

WHAT BUFFETT REALLY DID THAT YOU CAN DO

- He saved early and often
- He reinvested every dollar
- He let his money compound uninterrupted
- He avoided debt, distractions, and desperation

Buffett doesn't sell emotion. He sells time-tested principles:

- Buy what you understand
- Be greedy when others are fearful
- Let time multiply your consistency

Wisdom Of Overcoming

Wealth isn't about talent. It's not about luck. It's about timing and discipline.

You don't need a million today. But if you put $110, $250, $500, or $1,000 a week to work—with a plan—you can become the quiet owner of a million-dollar portfolio, while others flex credit and chase trends.

We're not building hype. We're building freedom. Because the more you own, the more time you control.

And the more time you control, the more you can live. Not survive. Not grind. Not flex. But live.

Chapter 43

Supply The Demand – 5 Real Life Stories Of Wealth Through Problem Solving

"Money doesn't chase people. It chases solutions."
— Daymond John

In every wealth empire, there is one root: someone saw a problem and had the guts, grit, or genius to solve it.

This chapter gives you five real-life stories—diverse in background, business, and strategy—but unified by one principle: Supply the demand.

Tristan Walker – Building Products for Black Skin and Beards
As a young Black man, Tristan Walker struggled with razor bumps and skin irritation. Every product on the shelf was designed for people with straight hair and smooth skin—not coarse, curly hair and melanin-rich skin.

He knew the demand existed. But no one was supplying real, science-backed, stylish solutions.

So he launched Bevel—a shaving and grooming system tailored specifically to Black men.

He faced pushback from VCs who didn't understand the market. He stayed focused.

He went direct-to-consumer. He used influencers before it was cool. He took pain and turned it into power.

Eventually, Procter & Gamble acquired Walker & Co., giving his vision global reach.

The demand: culturally specific grooming.
The solution: Bevel.
The result: a multi-million dollar exit and representation in every drugstore aisle that had ignored Black men for decades.

TIERRE FORD

Jayshree Ullal – Quietly Controlling the Cloud
While the world was fixated on social media and app startups, Jayshree Ullal—an Indian-born engineer—was quietly building the infrastructure behind the internet.

She became CEO of Arista Networks, supplying high-speed network switches for data centers.

In other words: when cloud giants like Google, Microsoft, and Facebook needed speed and power to grow, they called her.

Arista went public. The company reached a market cap of over $40 billion.

Jayshree owns over 5% of the company and became one of the richest self-made women in tech.

She didn't chase trends. She saw that the demand for data would grow forever—and she supplied the hardware to handle it.

Fred Swaniker – Educating the Next 1,000 Leaders of Africa
Fred Swaniker saw a future that terrified him: Africa rising in population but falling behind in leadership.

He didn't start a tech company. He started a school—The African Leadership Academy—then built a whole ecosystem around it.

Instead of focusing on top grades, he focused on critical thinking, entrepreneurial mindset, and civic responsibility.

His graduates didn't just get into Ivy League schools. They came back to build companies, change policy, and train others.

Fred is now building the African Leadership University network and the Room Fellowship.

He saw the demand: A future continent with talent but no training.
He built the supply: Schools that unlock leadership.

His impact isn't a dollar amount. It's the GDP of a generation.

Lisa Price – From Kitchen Experiments to a Beauty Powerhouse
In the 1990s, Lisa Price was a production assistant on TV sets in New

York. But in her small apartment, she began experimenting with essential oils, butters, and natural ingredients to create moisturizers and hair creams for herself and friends.

Most Black women at the time couldn't find affordable, natural, chemical-free beauty products that worked for their hair texture and skin tone.

So Lisa named her little project Carol's Daughter, after her own mother. She began selling at flea markets, street fairs, and by word of mouth.

The demand exploded.

By the early 2000s, she had opened a storefront in Brooklyn and built a direct-to-consumer base with loyal followers. Oprah and Jada Pinkett Smith co-signed. Steve Stoute helped scale the brand.

In 2014, L'Oréal acquired Carol's Daughter, giving Lisa Price a life-changing exit and securing a legacy in the beauty aisle that represented and respected Black women.

She didn't chase what was trending—she created what was missing.

Cathy Hughes – Radio Queen Who Gave Black America a Voice

Cathy Hughes didn't inherit a media company—she built one. Born in Omaha, Nebraska, and raised during segregation, she faced poverty, early motherhood, and rejection at nearly every step. But she had a vision: Black America needed its own microphone.

In the 1970s, she became the first woman to run a radio station at Howard University—WOL-AM. There, she flipped the script: instead of copying mainstream stations, she created "The Quiet Storm," a late-night show focused on R&B, real talk, and soul.

That show laid the foundation for her company: Radio One.

When she and her then-husband tried to buy their first station, 32 banks told them no. The 33rd said yes. After they divorced, Cathy bought out his half and slept in the station for months with her son while keeping it running.

Her model was revolutionary: serve underserved Black communities with content that reflected their lives—music, politics, pain, and power.

Radio One grew into Urban One, the largest African-American-owned broadcast media company in the U.S., with TV One, digital platforms, and over 50 stations nationwide.

Cathy became the first Black woman to head a publicly traded media company.

She didn't just supply a product. She supplied a platform for a people.

The problem: No one was speaking to Black America through media that reflected its truth.
Her solution: Build the stage. Then hand others the mic.

Chapter 44

Execution, Automation, And Mastery – Winning The War For Your Wealth

"Wealth isn't given. It's taken, protected, and earned through execution. This is war—economic war." — Anonymous

At this point in the journey, you've built the vision, planted the seeds, and started watching your assets grow. But growth —taxes, inflation, and policy shifts.

You've built. Now it's time to fortify and command.

1. Wealth Is War – Guarding Against Inflation, Policy, And Economic Erosion

Every dollar you earn is under attack.

Inflation eats your buying power.

Government policy rewrites the rules.

Tax laws shift. Markets swing. Currencies weaken.

This is why you can't just have wealth—you must protect it like a general guards his territory.

A. Combat Inflation

Hold assets that outpace inflation: real estate, dividend stocks, commodity ETFs (like gold or energy)

Consider Series I Bonds, TIPS (Treasury Inflation-Protected Securities), or short-duration bond ladders

Reinvest dividends so gains compound over rising cost cycles

B. Anticipate Policy Risk

Don't get caught unaware. Pay attention to:

Capital gains tax law changes

Real estate 1031 exchange restrictions

Retirement account limits and Roth conversion rules

Proactive tax planning (with your CPA and attorney) saves six to seven figures over time

C. Hedge Currency Exposure

Use international ETFs or foreign bank accounts (legally structured)

Consider holding crypto or gold as currency alternatives

Diversify income across borders, business types, and assets

2. Automate Execution – Set The System To Self-Manage

You can't scale or protect what you constantly micromanage.

Automation ensures the machine runs even when you're not watching.

A. Auto-Investing

Set weekly contributions into ETFs, Roth IRAs, or custodial accounts

Use M1 Finance, Fidelity, or Vanguard automation tools

B. Auto-Paying & Saving

Set auto-draft for taxes, debt payments, and insurance

Route income through a control account, then distribute it weekly or biweekly into investment buckets

C. Auto-Rebalancing

Rebalancing keeps your risk aligned

Use robo-advisors or quarterly check-ins with a portfolio manager

Automation isn't lazy—it's leverage.

3. Mastery – Becoming The Commander, Not Just The Creator

Most people stop once the income flows in. But true mastery begins once you:

Systematize your empire

Outsource your low-value decisions

Schedule wealth reviews with professionals quarterly

Track net worth monthly, annually, and by generation

Protect assets through insurance, legal shields, and firewalls

Mastery looks like:

A family office or virtual team that updates you

Dashboards that let you monitor, adjust, and scale

A personal wealth SOP (Standard Operating Procedure)

Backup plans for every stream you've built

Because commanders don't guess. They assess, adjust, and dominate.

Wisdom of Overcoming

You can't fight economic war with opinions. You fight it with execution, automation, and cold-blooded strategy.

Money never sleeps—but it does move. The only question is: will it move for you, or against you?

Protect your system.

Automate your process.

Master your structure.

Because the greatest wealth is not what you build. It's what you keep, control, and pass forward.

Chapter 45

The 4-Quarter Wealth Review – Annual Assessments & Strategic Pivots

"What gets measured gets improved. What gets ignored gets erased." — Peter Drucker

If you've built streams, positioned assets, and automated your money, there's one last critical habit to master: the quarterly wealth review.

This isn't just about numbers. It's about steering the ship, adjusting to storms, and capitalizing on momentum.

WHY QUARTERLY REVIEWS MATTER

Wealth isn't a straight line. It shifts based on:

- Markets
- Policy changes
- Income swings
- Personal health or lifestyle transitions

Reviewing once a year is like driving cross-country with no map until the final mile. Quarterly reviews let you pivot early.

They help you:

- Track growth vs. projections
- Catch leaks or underperformance
- Adjust risk before losses compound
- Align money with mission

QUARTER 1 – FOUNDATION & FORECAST

Focus: Infrastructure, protection, and annual setup.

- Review all bank accounts, investment accounts, insurance policies

- Reconfirm trust documents, LLC status, and estate plan access

- Verify beneficiaries and emergency contact details

- Set your annual contribution goals: Roth IRA, 401(k), brokerage, etc.

- Forecast business revenue, W-2 income, and passive income goals

- Define ONE big wealth move (e.g., buy property, start a business, launch a fund)

This quarter is about cleaning the pipes before pouring more water through them.

QUARTER 2 – CASHFLOW & CAPITAL MOVEMENT

Focus: Liquidity, income flow, and ROI tracking.

- Review all incoming streams: salary, rent, dividends, royalties, side income

- Compare cashflow goals to actuals

- Identify any idle capital (large checking balances, unallocated cash)

- Reinvest dividends, idle funds, or debt paydown strategies

- Review credit score and debt strategy (optimize, consolidate, or reposition)

- Adjust tax withholding or estimated payments based on cashflow shifts

This is your engine check. Make sure the machine is flowing without friction.

QUARTER 3 – GROWTH & OPPORTUNITY ZONES

Focus: Expansion, rebalancing, and new opportunities.

- Rebalance portfolios (stocks, ETFs, crypto, real estate)

- Analyze investment performance (YTD and trailing 12-month)

- Identify lagging assets or holdings to replace

- Seek new placements: syndications, real estate, private equity, international options

- Attend one mastermind, wealth summit, or strategic meeting

- Explore educational investments (courses, licenses, hiring a coach)

This is where you pivot to power. What got you here may not get you to the next level.

QUARTER 4 – LEGACY, GIVING & YEAR-END STRATEGY

Focus: Protection, succession, and purpose.

- Max out contributions: Roth, SEP, 401(k), HSA, 529s

- Review charitable giving: Donor-Advised Fund, foundation, or direct gifts

- Execute end-of-year tax-loss harvesting if needed

- Confirm family meeting schedule or generational wealth strategy check-ins

- Audit trust activity and distributions

- Define next-year vision and close strong

End strong. Don't just survive the year. Use the fourth quarter to set up the next level.

SAMPLE DASHBOARD METRICS TO TRACK EACH QUARTER

- Net worth change (quarter vs. year-start)

- Passive income total (monthly + YTD)

- Investment ROI and asset allocation

- Liquidity ratio (cash vs. debt)

- Contribution status (Roth, HSA, brokerage)

- Estate update status (trusts, beneficiaries, insurance)

HOW TO AUTOMATE THIS PROCESS

- Use Google Sheets or Excel with formulas and pre-set charts

- Meet with CPA, advisor, or wealth team every 90 days

- Set calendar alerts to block 1 day per quarter for review

- Tie financial reviews to personal goals: fitness, family, faith, freedom

Wisdom Of Overcoming

You can't grow what you don't track. You can't protect what you don't audit. And you can't pass on what you don't master.

The Four-Quarter Wealth Review is how you shift from income to intent. From cash to command.

This is how you stop drifting and start driving.

Because real wealth is measured in freedom, power, and legacy.
And all three require you to watch the board, move the pieces, and control the outcome.

Chapter 46

Scaling With Partnership And Capital Stacking – Building The Empire To Last

"If you want to go fast, go alone. If you want to go far, go together—but fund it smart." — African Proverb (adapted)

Building wealth is one phase. Scaling it? That's a different game.
And no empire scales on the back of one person alone.

In this chapter, we break down the two secret weapons of sustainable scale:

1. Strategic Partnerships

2. Capital Stacking

This is how you stop building by force and start growing by formula.

PART 1: STRATEGIC PARTNERSHIPS – POWER THROUGH PEOPLE

You don't need a hundred employees.
You need a few people who:

- Share your vision
- Complement your weaknesses
- Bring leverage, not labor

Types of Strategic Partners:

A. Operational Partners
Run day-to-day, manage systems, hire talent, track metrics.
Let you focus on growth and vision.

B. Capital Partners
Bring money to the table. May take equity or a percentage of profit.
Perfect for real estate, franchising, or digital brands.

C. Distribution Partners
Already have your audience or customer.

You plug into their system.
Example: selling your product through someone else's list, storefront, or platform.

D. Licensing Partners
Use your brand or IP. They pay you.
Great for scaling content, courses, tech, or product formulas.

How to Choose the Right Partner:

- Trust but contract everything
- Shared vision, clear lanes
- Exit plan from Day 1
- If equity, make it performance-based

Ask: What do they reduce, replace, or accelerate? If they don't do one, they're not a partner. They're an employee.

PART 2: CAPITAL STACKING – MULTIPLE LAYERS OF FUNDING

When you're ready to scale—buy bigger, launch faster, go wider—you'll need capital.
But smart builders never rely on one source.

They use a capital stack.

What is a Capital Stack?

A mix of funding sources:

- Cash (yours or partners')
- Bank loans
- Private equity or angel investors
- Revenue-based financing
- Grants or crowdfunding
- Seller financing (in acquisitions)
- Credit lines or equipment leasing

Each layer plays a role:

- Equity = long-term fuel

- Debt = short-term speed
- Grants = free power
- Revenue-based = flexible flow

Stacking gives you optionality.
And control.

Example: Buying a $1M Asset (Real Estate or Business)

- $100K cash from you
- $150K private investor at 10% return
- $600K bank loan
- $150K seller financing

Now you control a million-dollar asset without burning all your capital. You split profits. You own equity. And your exposure is spread, not stacked on your back.

Mindset For Scale

You can't scale with scarcity. You must think in terms of systems, teams, and capital.

Ask yourself:

- What can I automate or delegate?
- What capital do I control vs. what can I access?
- What deal would 10x my world if I had the right partners?

COMMON MISTAKES TO AVOID

- Giving up too much equity too soon
- Not having clear agreements in writing
- Partnering with people just because they have money (but no alignment)
- Using short-term debt for long-term plays
- Not planning the exit before the entry

WISDOM OF OVERCOMING

You were never meant to build it all alone. You were meant to orchestrate, not just operate.

Partnership gives you reach.
Capital stacking gives you runway.
Together, they give you scale without sacrifice.

You don't just want a business. You want an empire.
And empires are built with layers.

Chapter 47

From Passive To Purpose – Philanthropic Legacy Work

"The goal isn't just to get rich—it's to give rich, live full, and leave a mark that money alone can't measure."
— Anonymous

At some point in the wealth journey, the game changes.

You no longer hustle for survival. You no longer invest just to build. Now, you're asking deeper questions:

- What does this all mean?
- Who am I helping beyond my family?
- What happens when I'm gone?

This is the pivot from passive income to purposeful impact. From stacking cash to shaping culture. From personal wealth to philanthropic legacy.

Let's build that system.

PART 1: THE PURPOSE PIVOT – FROM INCOME TO IMPACT

When your streams are flowing and your assets are protected, you reach a new threshold:

You have enough.

The next step is to convert excess into impact—not randomly, but strategically.

Ask:

- What injustice bothers you the most?
- What helped you that you now want to fund for others?
- What future do you want your name tied to?

This isn't charity. This is *legacy architecture*.

PART 2: STRUCTURES FOR GIVING

1. Donor-Advised Fund (DAF)

- Easy to set up with Schwab, Fidelity, or Vanguard
- You contribute, get an immediate tax deduction, and distribute to charities over time
- Great for families to learn how to give together

2. Private Family Foundation

- More control and branding
- Set your mission, board members (family), and funding plan
- Annual reports required, but you decide what gets funded, when, and how
- Can employ family members for admin, program design, etc.

3. Charitable Trusts

- Combine giving with wealth transfer
- CRTs (Charitable Remainder Trusts) pay you income now, then donate what's left later
- Great for reducing estate taxes while keeping lifetime cashflow

4. Direct Giving & Impact Funds

- Fund local schools, shelters, scholarships, or churches directly
- Invest in social enterprises or ESG funds that align with your values

PART 3: LEGACY TEAM MEETINGS

Hold a family "Purpose Session" annually:

- Review giving as a team
- Let children help choose causes
- Teach them how to vet charities
- Draft a "Legacy Statement" to attach to your trust

This becomes your family mission—not just your money map.

PART 4: MINDSET SHIFT – FROM PHILANTHROPY TO POWER

This isn't just about being generous. This is about shaping the world.

- Wealth gave you voice
- Purpose gives you volume

- Systems give you structure

When you combine the three, you become something bigger than a business owner. You become a legacy leader.

Wisdom Of Overcoming

You didn't come this far to flex.

You came to fund what matters. To fix what's broken. To build what you wish had existed when you were coming up.

This chapter isn't about giving what's left.

It's about leading with what lasts.

Chapter 48

The Ultimate Asset – Monetizing Pain, Power & Purpose

"Everything you survived is a blueprint. Every scar is a signature.
Turn your pain into power. Then turn that power into product."
— Unknown

This is the chapter where everything comes full circle.

You've earned. You've invested. You've automated. You've protected. You've given.

But now we ask: What's the one thing no one else has but you?

Your story. Your struggle. Your strength. Your perspective. Your journey.

Pain is an asset.
Power is a message.
Purpose is a model.

And when structured correctly, they become income streams, legacy engines, and transformational brands.

PART 1: PAIN IS PROOF YOU SURVIVED – NOW PACKAGE IT

Every setback, heartbreak, and trap you escaped isn't just a chapter in your life.
It's a case study, curriculum, or consulting angle.

Ask:

- What did I overcome that others are still stuck in?

- What system did I build to survive?

- What would I teach my younger self?

This becomes:

- A course

- A coaching program

- A keynote speech

- A memoir

- A nonprofit curriculum

You are the asset. Now position it.

PART 2: POWER IS IN POSITIONING – BUILD THE PLATFORM

You've built something others admire. Now make it a platform.

Examples:

- A former addict turns recovery into a mobile rehab app

- A single mom builds a community for financial literacy and launches a membership site

- A formerly incarcerated entrepreneur turns his time served into reentry training and wins corporate contracts

What you've lived through isn't random. It's raw material for your brand.

Use tools like:

- Substack or Medium for long-form thought leadership

- YouTube or Podcasting for building trust

- Gumroad or Kajabi to sell digital products

- Shopify or print-on-demand for branded goods

Document the journey. Package the wisdom.
Build a business from what they thought would break you.

PART 3: PURPOSE INTO PROFIT – SYSTEMIZE YOUR IMPACT

You don't need to go viral. You need to go deep.

Create a system:

- Capture attention: lead magnet or story

- Convert pain: show how you overcame

- Deliver solution: product, service, message

Example Model: "I used to _____, now I help others _____ using _____."

Ex: "I used to be $80K in debt, now I help single mothers build $10K emergency funds using my 3-part budgeting method."

The pain becomes the hook.
The power becomes the bridge.
The purpose becomes the product.

PART 4: MULTIPLE WAYS TO MONETIZE YOUR MESSAGE

- Courses & Ebooks: Sell your method step-by-step
- Consulting & Speaking: Offer transformation live or 1-on-1
- Subscriptions: Charge for community access, tools, or accountability
- Workshops: Virtual or in-person intensives
- Licensing: Let others teach your method and pay you

You're not just building a brand.
You're building a belief system with value.

WISDOM OF OVERCOMING

What hurt you was real.
But what you do with it? That's your legacy.

You don't just get paid for what you do.
You get paid for what you've been through—if you package the lesson.

So stop hiding the chapters that broke you.
Start publishing them.

Because your voice is your vault.
And your pain was never the end.

It was the foundation for your ultimate asset.

Chapter 49

The Blueprint Repeats – From $50k To $50m

"If you can scale $50K the right way, you can scale $50M the same way—just with more zeros and less emotion." — Anonymous

We've walked the journey from surviving to scaling, from hustling to automating, from cashflow to control.

This chapter reminds you: the blueprint doesn't change—just the size of the board.

The same principles that helped you grow $50K into $500K... and that $500K into $5M... are the same principles that build $50 million.

The wealth game has levels, but it's still chess. Same board. New strategy.

THE STAGES OF THE BLUEPRINT

STAGE 1: SURVIVAL TO STRUCTURE ($50K to $250K)

- Build discipline with $100–$500/week investing
- Eliminate high-interest debt
- Protect income with insurance and budget automation
- Start building ownership: small business, side hustle, or real estate entry

STAGE 2: STRUCTURE TO SCALING ($250K to $1M)

- Use leverage wisely (good debt)
- Increase contribution capacity with higher income or business growth
- Systematize wealth flow: investments, taxes, insurance, tracking
- Acquire scalable assets (multi-unit real estate, digital assets, franchises)

STAGE 3: SCALING TO STRATEGY ($1M to $10M)

- Install team: CPA, wealth advisor, attorney, assistant
- Execute capital stack strategies: equity, lending, fundraising
- Focus on risk-adjusted growth: venture capital, commercial real estate, business acquisition

- Create systems that print cashflow without your labor

STAGE 4: STRATEGY TO EMPIRE ($10M to $50M)

- Shift into legacy operating mode
- Build holding companies and permanent capital vehicles
- Launch funds, invest through trust entities, and sit on cap tables
- Influence markets, not just participate in them

Every stage requires the same tools: structure, discipline, vision, strategy.

The only thing that changes is how far ahead you see.

PRINCIPLES THAT NEVER CHANGE

- Pay yourself first
- Buy what pays you
- Protect the downside
- Track everything
- Keep cashflow king
- Stay legally armored

Whether you manage $5,000 or $50,000,000—those rules stay firm.

REPEATING THE BLUEPRINT IN EVERY AREA

Real Estate:

- First rental becomes 10 doors, becomes 100-unit portfolio

Business:

- First side hustle becomes a company, becomes a multi-brand ecosystem

Investments:

- First ETF becomes Roth + brokerage + trust portfolio with $1M in dividends

Legacy:

- First giving moment becomes DAF, then foundation, then family office with its own board

You don't change the playbook—you just upgrade the players and the field.

Wisdom Of Overcoming

The blueprint is not about luck. It's not even about income.

It's about how you stack decisions over time.

Every investment was a seed. Every pivot was a strategy. Every system was a gear in your machine.

You can do it again. And again. And again.

Because wealth isn't a destination.
It's a blueprint that repeats.

And now—it's yours system.

Chapter 50

Traits Of Winners & The Compounding Parable – Choosing The Better Million

"Discipline is the bridge between goals and accomplishment."
— Jim Rohn

20 Traits and Habits of Winners

1. Discipline – They show up daily, not just when it's convenient.

2. Vision – They start with the end in mind.

3. Consistency – They repeat small wins until momentum takes over.

4. Patience – They trust the process over the pace.

5. Curiosity – They keep learning, adapting, and questioning.

6. Execution – They act while others are still planning.

7. Grit – They outlast the noise.

8. Focus – They eliminate distractions.

9. Humility – They remain teachable.

10. Confidence – They trust their preparation.

11. Faith – They believe before results show.

12. Systems Thinking – They use processes, not passion alone.

13. Emotional Intelligence – They manage energy and reactions.

14. Adaptability – They pivot without panic.

15. Time Mastery – Every hour is accounted for.

16. Goal Setting – They know where they're going.

17. Financial Literacy – They speak money's language.

18. Resilience – They bounce back harder.

19. Network Cultivation – They invest in people.

20. Delayed Gratification – They play the long game.

The Parable: A Million Now or a Penny That Doubles?

Imagine this choice:

- Get $1 million right now, no strings.
- Or take 1 penny that doubles every day for 30 days.

Most would grab the million. But here's how the penny adds up:

- Day 1: $0.01
- Day 5: $0.16
- Day 10: $5.12
- Day 15: $163.84
- Day 20: $5,242.88
- Day 25: $167,772.16
- Day 28: $1.34 million
- Day 30: $5.36 million

The lesson? Compounding is quiet at first—then explosive.

This is why consistent investing, daily discipline, and wise decisions multiply far beyond short-term grabs.

Final Encouragement: Getting Started Wins

You don't need a fancy plan.
You don't need $10,000 saved up.
You just need to begin.

Even if it's small. Even if you're uncertain. Even if you feel behind.

Because every winner, every investor, every empire began the same way: with a first step.

And if you repeat that step daily—stacking time, learning, money, and faith?

You become unstoppable.

Because the richest force on earth is not gold.
 It's compounding.

So get started.

You've got the blueprint.
 Now let it build you back. workshops.

Epilogue

From Shoebox To Empire – The Blueprint Was You

We started with shoebox money.
Hustling to stay afloat. Stashing cash in corners, dodging risk,
surviving the moment.

But now?

Now you're a wealth builder.
Same drive. Same hustle. But with a blueprint behind it.
Now every dollar moves with strategy. Every stream has a system. Every setback became study.

What made the difference?

Planning. Discipline. The compound effect.

Once you understand that passive income is the real king—and that sitting cash is dead cash—your entire outlook shifts.
You stop chasing.
You start commanding.

That's when the empire begins.

And the most beautiful part?
It never mattered where you started.
It mattered that you started.
Half the battle is beginning. The other half is consistency with the right information.

Wealth isn't built in emotion.
It's built in systems, seasons, and silence.
While others shout, you build.
While others spend, you plant.
While others flex, you scale.

So here you are.
A new architect of abundance.

Not just for you—but for your bloodline, your community, and your purpose.

Patience wins.
Compounding wins.
The right information wins 90% of the battle.

The other 10%?
That's your decision to act.

This wasn't just a book.
This was a blueprint.
And now—it's yours to run.

CLOSING STORIES – FIVE REAL LIVES THAT BUILT LEGACIES

"Don't let your zip code trap your vision. Don't let your pain bury your potential. Every one of these names started with less than you might think—and turned it into a blueprint the world couldn't ignore."

As we close this book, let's anchor the lessons in real lives, real names, and real transformation. These five stories are more than success tales— they're proof that with vision, discipline, and purpose, you can scale anything.

1. Ray Dalio – From Job Loss to Building the Largest Hedge Fund on Earth

Ray Dalio didn't come from generational wealth. Raised in a modest Long Island neighborhood, he started investing at age 12—not because someone handed him millions, but because he was curious and willing to learn.

After working on Wall Street, he launched Bridgewater Associates out of a two-bedroom apartment. In 1982, he predicted a global depression— and got it wrong. So wrong, he lost clients, staff, and credibility. He had to borrow $4,000 just to make rent.

But he didn't quit. He rebuilt Bridgewater on transparency, radical truth, and deep systems.

Today, Bridgewater manages over $150 billion. Dalio is a billionaire several times over and known for his writing (*Principles*) and philanthropy.

His pain taught him humility. His rebuilding taught him discipline. His purpose taught him patience.

2. Coach K & Pee – Building Quality Control from Culture, Not Corporations

Kevin "Coach K" Lee and Pierre "Pee" Thomas weren't born into music empires. They were born into Atlanta streets—where talent was everywhere but platforms were rare.

Instead of begging record labels, they built one. Quality Control Music started in a modest studio, managing the careers of local artists who didn't fit the industry mold.

They understood culture better than executives in suits ever could. That insight led to the rise of Migos, Lil Baby, City Girls, Lil Yachty, and others.

QC's empire scaled through brand deals, ownership stakes, and expansion. In 2023, they sold a majority share for $300 million, but retained influence, control, and their brand identity.

They flipped community into capital. Vision into volume.
They didn't wait for the industry—they became it.

3. Master P – From Food Stamps to Empire Builder

Percy Miller, known as Master P, was raised in the Calliope Projects of New Orleans. His family was on welfare. He didn't have a mentor. What he had was hunger—and the discipline to learn the game.

After receiving a $10,000 life insurance settlement from his grandfather's death, he opened a record store. He didn't just sell music—he studied distribution, pricing, marketing.

He eventually turned No Limit Records into one of the most profitable labels of the '90s—earning 80% of his revenue while other artists only got crumbs.

P didn't stop at music. He launched:

- Clothing lines
- Real estate plays
- Food products (Rap Snacks, Uncle P's)
- Films, sports management, and tech

Today, Master P is a multi-hundred-million-dollar mogul—all from knowing his audience and building vertically.

His lesson: own everything you touch. Build the ladder instead of waiting for someone to lower one.

4. John Hope Bryant – The Architect of Financial Uplift

Born in South Central LA, John Hope Bryant was a teenage entrepreneur—cutting lawns, selling candy, and watching his family struggle with financial systems designed to exclude them.

Instead of getting bitter, he got strategic.

He founded Operation HOPE, a nonprofit focused on economic empowerment in underserved communities. He pioneered financial literacy for the streets, launching banking centers inside barbershops, schools, and churches.

He also became a force behind U.S. Treasury initiatives and civil rights economic policy.

His idea was simple: you can't fix social injustice without economic power.
He taught millions how to:

- Raise credit scores
- Start businesses
- Protect assets
- Create generational plans

John Hope Bryant became the go-to financial voice for presidents, CEOs, and everyday hustlers alike.

He reminds us: Credit is power. Literacy is freedom. Wealth is strategy.

5. Asa Candler – The Coke That Took Over the World

The founder of Coca-Cola wasn't the original inventor of the drink.
But Asa Candler was the one who saw its potential.

He bought the secret formula from a struggling pharmacist for just $2,300 in the late 1800s.

What did he do next?

- Built a distribution system across states
- Gave away branded items—calendars, coupons, glassware—to seed awareness

- Invested in bottling infrastructure before the world caught up

By 1900, Coca-Cola wasn't just a drink. It was a lifestyle brand.
He made millions.
His descendants turned it into billions.

The lesson?
It's not about inventing something new.
It's about recognizing value early, owning it, and distributing it with consistency.

FINAL WISDOM

Five people.
Five paths.
Five proof points that wealth is never about where you start. It's about what you build—and how long you stay in the game.

You have the vision.
Now you have the tools.

The rest is just execution, alignment, and time.

OTHER BOOKS BY TIERRE FORD

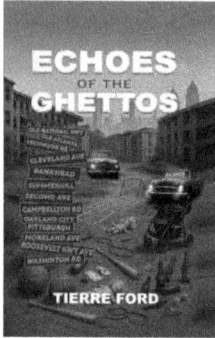

ECHOES OF THE GHETTOS — TIERRE FORD

GHOST DOPE — TIERRE FORD

THE GREAT RESET — Echo Of The Achitect — TIERRE FORD

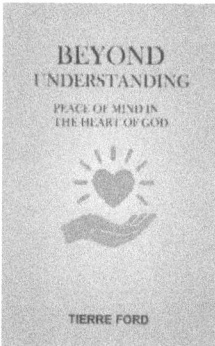

BEYOND UNDERSTANDING — PEACE OF MIND IN THE HEART OF GOD — TIERRE FORD

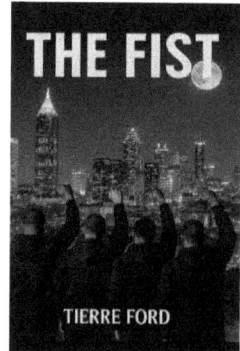

THE FIST — TIERRE FORD

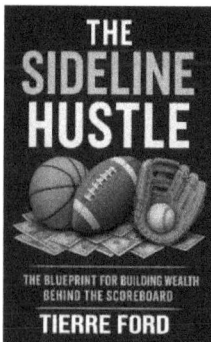

THE SIDELINE HUSTLE — THE BLUEPRINT FOR BUILDING WEALTH BEHIND THE SCOREBOARD — TIERRE FORD

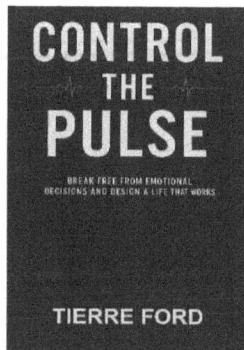

CONTROL THE PULSE — BREAK FREE FROM EMOTIONAL DECISIONS AND DESIGN A LIFE THAT WORKS — TIERRE FORD

2+2=8 — Plant The Seeds, Watch Them Grow — TIERRE FORD

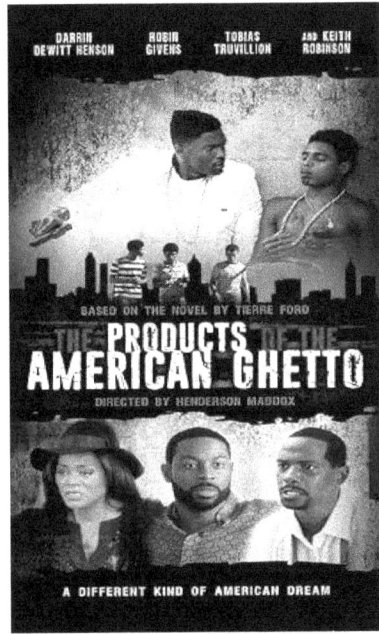

TIERRE FORD

www.ingramcontent.com/pod-product-compliance
Lightning Source LLC
Chambersburg PA
CBHW061020220326
41597CB00016BB/1729